For my family and friends, who never gave up on me.
I wouldn't be where I am today without their
continued love and support.

IF
YOU
LOVE
ME

IF
YOU
LOVE
ME

True love.

True terror.

True story.

ALICE KEALE
WITH JANE SMITH

HARPER
element

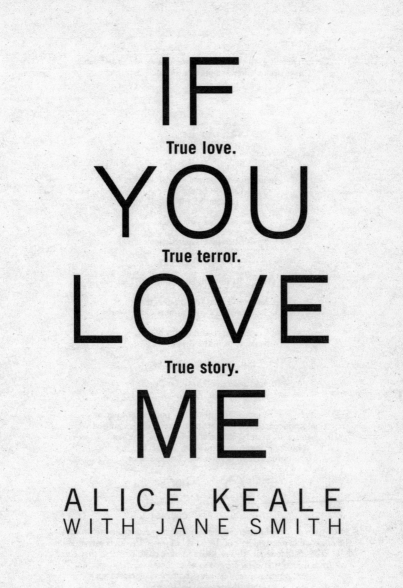

Certain details in this story, including names, places and dates, have been changed to protect the family's privacy.

HarperElement
An imprint of HarperCollins*Publishers*
1 London Bridge Street
London SE1 9GF

www.harpercollins.co.uk

First published by HarperElement 2017

1 3 5 7 9 10 8 6 4 2

© Alice Keale with Jane Smith 2017

Alice Keale and Jane Smith assert the moral
right to be identified as the authors of this work

A catalogue record of this book is
available from the British Library

ISBN 978-0-00-820525-6

Printed and bound in Great Britain by
Clays Ltd, St Ives plc

MIX
Paper from
responsible sources
FSC™ www.fsc.org   FSC™ C007454

FSC™ is a non-profit international organisation established to promote
the responsible management of the world's forests. Products carrying the
FSC label are independently certified to assure customers that they come
from forests that are managed to meet the social, economic and
ecological needs of present and future generations,
and other controlled sources.

Find out more about HarperCollins and the environment at
www.harpercollins.co.uk/green

Prologue

I glanced down at the luminous hands of the large watch
that made my wrist look as thin as a child's. Surely that
couldn't be the right time. It couldn't possibly have taken
me as long as that just to get this far. Then I remembered
that he'd set the watch before I left, so I knew it was accu-
rate. Which meant that I would have to run even faster if
I was going to reach the pub, take a photograph on his
mobile phone and get back to the house in the few minutes
that remained before time ran out.

Quickening my pace, I scanned the darkness of every
side street and every shop doorway I passed. And I listened
too, for the sound of approaching footsteps or distant
voices.

As I ran past the café where we had sat together just a
few hours earlier, I thought I saw a flicker of movement,
and the ever-present knot of fear tightened inside me. It
was almost 1 a.m. on a Wednesday night and I'd been

certain I was the only person out on the street. But, suddenly, a man stepped out of the shadows directly in front of me.

I had to swerve off the pavement and on to the road to avoid being caught in his outstretched arms, and as I did so I was engulfed in the alcohol-laden breath he exhaled when he lunged towards me. I gasped in shocked surprise, but kept on running, ignoring the sharp objects I could feel cutting into the flesh of my bare, bruised feet and the incoherent shouts of the man who stumbled after me down the dimly lit street.

I couldn't really blame him for pursuing me – a woman running naked through the streets of London in the middle of the night. Perhaps he thought I was playing some salacious game. It was certainly an explanation that would have made more sense than the real reason, which I didn't understand myself – and *I* was completely sober.

I was frightened of the drunk man, and of what he might do if he caught up with me. But I was even more frightened of what would happen if I didn't get home within the next three minutes. 'Maybe *this* time it will be enough,' I thought, as I ran, sobbing, through the darkness.

'Please, God,' I whispered into the night, 'let it be *this* time.'

Chapter 1

Although my love life was pretty much a disaster, things were going well at work and I'd managed to save enough money for a deposit on a flat of my own. So when my flatmate, Connie, went to live with her boyfriend, I arranged to rent the spare room in my friend Cara's flat until I could find somewhere to buy.

It was August 2011 and I was alone on what would be my last night in the rented flat Connie and I had shared. I'd already taken almost everything I was going to need in the short term to Cara's place and stored the rest in the garage at my parents' house in Devon. So all I had to do that evening was pack a small suitcase to take with me the next day. I was looking forward to buying a place of my own and starting the next phase of my life, and after having a nice dinner out with friends I was just thinking about heading off to bed for an early night when I heard the sound of breaking glass.

The flat was above some shops on quite a busy street, and my first thought was that there'd been a car accident. But what I saw when I looked out of the window was like a scene from a dystopian film. There were people running in every direction, most of them wearing hoodies and scarves that concealed their faces and some of them hurling what looked like bricks and bottles through shop windows. At first, I couldn't make any sense of what was happening. Then, as I watched, with my back pressed against the wall beside the window so that I couldn't be seen, a group of people started rocking a car from side to side, before stumbling backwards when smoke began to curl around it and then flames exploded out of it.

I was shaking as I phoned the police. 'There's rioting all over London,' the police operator told me. 'So it might be some time before anyone gets there. Just stay in your flat. Whatever you do, don't go outside.'

I moved away from the window after speaking to her, and was crouched in the hallway when my phone rang. 'Dad and I have been listening to the news,' Mum said, sounding less worried than she would have done if she'd known the true situation. 'Is there rioting where you are?'

'It's fine,' I told her, walking from the hallway into my bedroom at the back of the flat and closing the door as I spoke, so that she wouldn't hear the sounds from the street.

I didn't know the neighbours, who'd only recently moved in to the flat next door. But after I'd reassured Mum, I knocked on their door and asked if I could sit with them for a while, because I didn't want to be on my own. Something had been thrown through their living-room window just a few minutes earlier, and after they'd shown me the shards of glass that covered the carpet we sat in their bedroom, as far away from the street as we could get, and waited for the police to arrive. In fact, things had already started to calm down a bit by the time they got there, and I decided to go back to my place and try to get a couple of hours' sleep.

It felt as though my head had only just touched the pillow when my phone rang again. It was Connie this time, and her voice was tight with anxiety as she asked, 'Are you in the flat, Alice? It's on TV. I'm watching it now. They've set fire to the shops underneath. You've got to get out.'

I'd been so tired I'd fallen into bed fully clothed and I was just grabbing my suitcase when there was a knock on the front door. The fireman who was standing there when I opened it told me, 'We're evacuating the building. They've fire-bombed the shop on the corner. You need to leave – now.' So I followed my neighbours out on to the smoke-filled street, where the last of the rioters were being herded past the burning buildings and around the corner by police.

Someone had opened up a café a few doors down from the flat, to provide a refuge for people who'd had to be evacuated from their homes. It was about four o'clock in the morning by that time, and all the other people there looked as exhausted and dazed as I felt. Fortunately, the fire didn't spread to my flat, and when the fire-fighters eventually got it under control, I was able to go back and try to sleep again for a couple of hours.

Someone from the letting agency was due to do an inventory later that morning, but I was so tired by the time he arrived that I left him to it. Cara was away for a couple of days, so she'd given me a key to let myself in to her flat, and although I had been planning to go there first to drop off my bag, being at work suddenly seemed like a much better option than sitting there on my own.

I worked at that time for a company that owned several art galleries, and when I emailed my boss to tell her what had happened and that I was going to be a bit late arriving at the office, she answered immediately, asking if I was all right and telling me to take the day off. I don't think what had happened had really sunk in by that time. The adrenaline was still pumping around my body and although I was incredibly tired and shocked I wasn't yet feeling particularly distressed, and my boss seemed to understand when I said I wanted to keep busy. So I did go in to work, and when I got there I was sitting at my desk talking to some of my colleagues about what had happened when Joe came over.

Joe held a senior position as head of a department at the company I worked for, and although I knew vaguely who he was I hadn't ever spoken to him before. 'I heard about your experience this morning,' he said. 'And I just wanted to make sure you were okay.' He seemed genuinely concerned, so I assured him that I was fine, apart from being tired and finding it a bit difficult to process what I'd seen – the overturned cars, smashed windows, looted shops and people running riot through the streets. 'I still think you need to go home,' he said. 'You've had a shock and when it catches up with you, home is the best place for you to be.'

He was right about the shock catching up with me. The adrenaline was already starting to subside and, as it did so, I was overcome by an almost paralysing weariness. So Joe got me a taxi, which the company paid for, and half an hour later I let myself in to Cara's flat, with barely minutes to spare before exhaustion finally kicked in.

I sent Joe an email before I fell into bed, thanking him for the taxi and telling him he'd been right about home being the best place, which he answered immediately, saying, 'It's fine. Don't worry about it. Just have a good rest. Joe X.'

I don't sign off emails or texts with a kiss, except to family and close friends. But I know a lot of people do. So it probably wouldn't have seemed particularly odd that Joe had done so if it hadn't been for our relative positions at work and for the fact that we'd only spoken to each other for the first time that morning – although I was too weary to wonder about it by then.

I had just finished reading Joe's email when Cara's mum phoned to check that I'd been able to get into the flat and that everything was okay. It was while I was talking to her that the impact of the whole traumatic experience finally hit me and I had to end the call because I couldn't stop sobbing. Then I went to bed and slept without waking until the following morning.

Joe made a point of coming to see me the next day, to ask if I was feeling better and if I'd managed to sleep. He sat on the edge of my desk in the large open-plan office for about half an hour, talking about what had happened and studying the diagram he asked me to draw to show exactly where the flat was in relation to where the rioting had kicked off in the street below.

Part of my job involved setting up exhibitions of paintings and sculpture at various galleries around the country, and although I hadn't had any direct contact with Joe before then, he was ultimately responsible for my team. So there was nothing unusual in the fact that we were both included in the emails that were sent round to everyone a couple of days later suggesting we should all meet up for a drink after work one evening. We didn't get the chance to talk to each other on that occasion, however, because I was held up at the office and didn't make it to the bar until after Joe had left.

Meanwhile, what only a determined optimist would have referred to as my 'love life' was barely ticking over. Anthony, the married man I was 'seeing', had only been to my flat once during the few weeks prior to the night of the riots. But, based on the emails and texts he occasionally sent me – and on a great deal of wishful thinking – I still considered myself to be in a relationship with him. Not that my situation with Anthony had any relevance to how I felt about Joe. Although Joe was friendly and seemed very pleasant, I wasn't interested in him in that way. So I was surprised to receive an email from him one day when I was doing some research in a large art gallery in London, asking if I'd like to meet for a quick coffee after work.

'Unfortunately, I can't,' I emailed back. 'I'm meeting some friends.'

His answer came almost immediately. 'That's a shame. I'm going to Berlin in the morning. I'll be away for a week. Of course, we could always meet there for coffee …!' To which I responded in the same jokey manner and was flattered when he suggested we should have a drink when he got back.

I did see him the following week, after his trip to Berlin, but he didn't say anything about the emails or about getting together for a drink. So I sent a text to my best friend, Sarah, asking whether she thought I should mention it to him, and she answered, 'Go for it! Just see what he's like. You've been really miserable and you deserve to be happy.' And when I texted Joe, he suggested meeting for a drink after work a few days later.

Apart from those few emails and texts, we'd only ever spoken to each other about work and the riots, so I don't know what I was expecting to happen when we did meet up. I still believed I loved Anthony, even though we saw each other only rarely by that time. But although I wasn't ready to admit it to myself yet, I think I already knew, on some level, that we weren't going to have a future together, and I often wished I could have the sort of normal, uncomplicated relationship with a nice, single guy that most of my friends had.

I'd only really had one serious relationship before I started seeing Anthony – which had lasted several years before we split up. So the prospect of having what seemed to be a date with Joe made me both nervous and excited. In fact, I was so agitated on the day itself that I barely ate anything, and as I made my way to the trendy, expensive club where he'd suggested we should meet, my stomach was rumbling noisily.

'Get a grip,' I told myself severely as I pushed my way through the almost solid tide of commuters heading in the opposite direction, towards the train station from which I'd just come. 'It isn't really a date. You're just meeting a man you barely know for a drink.' It was true that I knew almost nothing about Joe, except that he was clever and seemed to be universally liked and respected by his colleagues. But, for some reason, I'd been looking forward all day to what I kept reminding myself was just a casual drink.

I'd been delayed leaving work and was a few minutes late by the time I arrived at the club and climbed the stairs to the rooftop bar where I was due to meet Joe. There was still time to stop for a moment in front of the long mirror on the landing, though, and when I did so I was horrified by the red-faced, flustered-looking woman staring back at me. 'Well, that's a good start,' I told her. 'He's going to be thrilled when he sees you!' Then I imagined what he might say, which made me wonder, anxiously, what I would say to him. What would we talk about? What if he thought I was boring – as well as being an unattractive shade of puce and suffering from severe, and very audible, digestive problems? What if he made a quick excuse and fled as soon as he could do so without appearing to be downright rude?

'For heaven's sake, calm down,' I told the woman in the mirror, silently. 'You can do this. People don't normally dislike you. You can hold a conversation and have fun. You've got some really nice, intelligent friends who wouldn't bother with you if you were boring and stupid.

You just need to move away from the mirror now and believe that everything will be all right.'

When I stepped out on to the roof of the building a couple of seconds later, it was as if someone had suddenly turned up the volume on the muffled buzz of conversation that could be heard from inside. In fact, the bar was full of people, and as I scanned them in search of Joe I could feel the knot of anxiety tightening in my already protesting stomach. 'Perhaps he hasn't arrived yet,' I thought. 'Maybe something's kept him late at work. Maybe he won't come at all.'

Then I saw him, sitting on a sofa with his head bent over his phone. Just a split second later he looked up and saw me, and as his face broke into a smile the knot in my stomach unravelled and I suddenly felt completely calm. After that, even the awkward bit was easy – those seconds when you've spotted the person you're meeting but still have to cross the ground between you, not knowing whether to maintain eye contact and keep smiling inanely or look away until you're within hand-shaking or cheek-kissing distance.

Joe stood up when he saw me, and as soon as I was close enough to be able to hear him above the laughing chatter of the crowd he leaned forward and said into my ear, 'I've got you a drink already. A gin and tonic. I hope that's okay?'

'That's perfect,' I said, sinking on to the sofa beside him. 'Thanks. And hi.'

If You Love Me

On the relatively rare occasions when I go out on weekday evenings when I'm working, I don't stay out late. But Joe and I were still in the bar four hours later, laughing and talking as though we'd known each other for years. He was funny and charming, and the more we talked, the more struck we were by how much we seemed to have in common. Everything *I* liked, Joe liked – and had something interesting or insightful to say about it. We laughed at the same things, had the same list of countries we wanted to visit, admired the same people, loved the work of the same artists, had read or wanted to read the same books, had the same opinions about films we'd seen, and loved or loathed the same foods …

That first evening I spent with Joe was quite possibly the best evening of my entire life. I don't know whether I lacked self-confidence any more than anyone else, but I could hardly believe that someone like him could be so obviously attracted to someone like me. The hours just flew by, and when he leaned towards me, put his hands very gently on my cheeks and kissed me, it felt like coming home.

'I don't want this evening to end,' he said, voicing the thought that had been going through my mind for the last couple of hours. 'Will you come back to my place tonight? Let's agree not to have sex. Just come home with me – for a sleep-over.' Tiny lines radiated out from his eyes when he laughed. 'I just want to go to sleep knowing you'll be there when I wake up. I know it sounds crazy, but I think I want to spend the rest of my life with you, Alice. I've never felt this way before.'

And maybe it would have sounded crazy to anyone who might have been listening in the bar that night. But it sounded perfectly sane to me, and it didn't even cross my mind to say anything other than, 'Yes, I will go home with you. I feel exactly the same way. I can't explain it, but I feel as though I've known you for years, not just a few hours. I …' I can't remember now what I was going to say before Joe kissed me again and pushed every thought out of my head.

Agreeing to go home with Joe that night was completely out of character for me. That might sound unlikely in view of the fact that, of the few things you already know about me, one is that I was having an affair with a married man. But it's true. It was something I wouldn't even have dreamed of doing in normal circumstances, or if it hadn't felt as though everything in my life suddenly made sense.

Sitting in the bar that night with a nice, uncomplicated, charismatic, interesting single man with a good job and a great sense of humour, it felt as though I might find love in my love life after all. Even more important, perhaps, was the fact that, by the end of the evening, I didn't despise myself as much as I had done until then, because if someone like Joe could like me, there might be hope for me after all.

Sitting there with Joe that evening just felt right some-how. I'd met a lot of sleazy execs over the previous few years, the sort of creepy guys who prey on junior colleagues – people like Anthony, in fact, although I didn't realise that at the time. But it was clear that Joe wasn't the sort of person to take advantage of anyone. I'd heard people at work talking about how he'd helped a colleague who was going through a difficult time in his personal life and how if it hadn't been for Joe's intervention the man would have lost his job. 'He stuck his neck out for Barry when he didn't have to,' someone said. 'It's the sort of thing he does.' Everyone seemed to like him. And now, apparently, this genuine, kind, intelligent person liked me.

One of the many things Joe told me about himself that first evening was that he was married, although he and his wife had been separated for more years than they'd been together. 'We got married too young,' he told me. 'We didn't have any children and there wasn't any property to be divided up – we both have jobs that enable us to support ourselves more than adequately financially. So although we haven't seen each other for five or six years, we just never got around to divorcing.'

Then I told him about Jack – the boyfriend I'd lived with for several years after I left university and who had broken my heart – but not about Anthony, because I didn't want him to judge me or change his mind about liking me. In fact, by the end of that first evening Joe liking me was so important that I lied to him and said there hadn't been anyone since Jack. That's the trouble with doing something you know is wrong: you end up doing more wrong things – like lying, for example – because you don't want people to find out about it.

When we left the bar, we took a taxi back to Joe's immaculate terraced house in a tree-lined street in an expensive part of south-west London. We didn't have sex, as agreed. We just talked and talked into the early hours of the morning, more than I'd ever talked with anyone in my life before. And the more we talked, the more we found we had in common, and the more I felt as though I'd known Joe for years, which is the way he said he felt about me, too.

I don't believe the happy-ever-after love stories of Hollywood movies. But I did start to wonder that night if maybe sometimes they weren't as far-fetched as I'd always thought they were.

The next morning, Joe drove me to work, where I spent the rest of the day trying to concentrate on what I was supposed to be doing. And when sex was added to the agenda that evening, it was as perfect as every other aspect of our new relationship seemed to be.

For the next two weeks, we spent almost every night together. I was supposed to be flat hunting, which was why I'd been staying in my friend Cara's flat since the day of the riots, when I first spoke to Joe. So I didn't have much more than a suitcase full of clothes to transport when I moved in with him a couple of weeks after our first date at the bar. It sounds crazy now, to have taken such a major step after knowing him for such a short period of time. But it just felt right. Whatever we tell ourselves, I think most of us *do* hope we've got a soul mate out there somewhere and that one day we'll find each other and live happily ever after. So when you think you've actually met your soul mate, why would you wait?

Although Jack and I had been together for years and I did love him, at no time during the course of our relationship did I ever feel what I felt with Joe almost from day one. When Jack and I split up, I'd got involved with Anthony almost by accident, because I was hurt and lonely and had begun to wonder if anyone would ever care about me again. For the last couple of years before I met Joe, and particularly after Jack dumped me, I hadn't wanted to feel anything. Joe and I didn't tell people at work that we were seeing each other. But that was our choice – at least, I think it was ours, rather than his, although I can't really remember now. I did tell my friends, though, and was touched by how happy they were for me.

When I met Joe, it felt as though I'd been swept up by a whirlwind and that, suddenly, I had a future again. When we were together in the evenings we talked almost incessantly, and about everything, including when and where we would get married – 'I know the perfect place for our wedding,' Joe told me – where we would live, and how many children we would have.

The 'perfect place for our wedding' turned out to be a small town in France Joe had visited with his wife a couple of years after they'd got married. He described to me how he had stood on the steps of a church there one day during their holiday, looking out towards the mountains, and felt a sense of peace he'd never experienced before or since. 'I can't wait for you to see it,' he said. And I told him I couldn't wait either, while silently berating myself for wishing we could get married somewhere he hadn't already visited with the wife he would first have to divorce.

Chapter 2

A lot of people have to deal with bad situations in their lives, and the things that had gone wrong for me before I met Joe weren't really that bad at all, in the greater scheme of things.

The first time there was any indication that something might be wrong was during my second year at university. I'd had glandular fever, so for a while I thought that was why I was tearful and felt so low. But when all the other symptoms finally cleared up and I was still miserable for no apparent reason, the doctor diagnosed depression.

Fortunately, the antidepressants I was given worked well. So well, in fact, that I eventually decided it had just been an isolated incident and I stopped taking them. And then, of course, the depression came back. It was disappointing to have to face the fact that it hadn't been 'cured' after all, and it was frustrating every time it recurred over the next few years. I was lucky, though, because it wasn't ever bad enough to interfere with my life to any significant extent and I never had to be hospitalised.

I was doing a degree in the history of art when I had the first episode of depression, and I was lucky again in that it didn't disrupt my studies and I was able to go on to finish my course. After my BA, I did a Masters degree, then worked as a temp for a while, before doing an internship at an auction house and eventually getting a job in an art gallery. A couple of years later, I was promoted within the same company and started earning a reasonable salary, which enabled me to pay to see a psychiatrist privately every few months, for reassurance as much as anything else.

I had all the usual insecurities and doubts most young people have about being 'good enough', but I had a good social life, was doing a job I enjoyed and, thanks largely to the tablets and to some cognitive behavioural therapy – which I found really useful – rarely had to take a day off work because of depression. So, apart from my family and the close friends who knew about my experience at university, no one was aware that there had ever been anything wrong with me at all.

The company I was working for had galleries and offices in numerous cities around the UK and abroad, and I was moved around a bit for the first couple of years after I was promoted, although only ever to places in England. By the time I started working on a more permanent basis in London, I'd been going out with my boyfriend Jack for almost four years.

Jack worked in an advertising agency in the Midlands and came to London most weekends to stay with me at the flat I shared with a friend from university. He planned to move down permanently as soon as the right job came up, and we were saving to buy a flat together. In fact, we'd begun to talk about getting married, and then he came to London one Friday evening and told me it was over.

Looking back on it now, I think that if Jack had already got a job in London our relationship might have ended sooner. We'd been together for seven years when he broke it off, and although we were comfortable in each other's company, people change in their twenties, and in reality we no longer had very much in common and had been drifting apart. It was only because we didn't see each other every day that we hadn't noticed that was the case – although I realise, in retrospect, that Jack must have been more aware of it than I was.

It's much easier to rationalise things when you look back on them from the distance of a few years than it is when you've just been dumped, and when Jack dumped me I was completely heartbroken. 'Can't we try to make it work?' I kept pleading with him that Friday evening. But he'd made up his mind and nothing I could say was going to change it. He did try to be kind, though, and because he knew the break-up would come as a complete bolt from the blue to me and I'd be very upset, he'd arranged for my mum to be in London that weekend. He must have texted her before he left my flat, a couple of hours after he'd broken the news to me, because she turned up just a few minutes later.

I know Mum was worried about me and that she really did want to help. But there was probably nothing she could have said that would have reduced the impact of what felt almost like a physical blow. I was in a state of shock and certainly didn't believe her when she told me everything was going to be okay and that I'd feel better about it all in a few days. I was twenty-nine years old, had believed Jack and I would be together for the rest of our lives, and just wanted to be left alone with my grief. So Mum went home the next morning, and I spent the rest of the weekend on my own in the flat, crying until I ran out of tears.

I didn't want to go into work on the Monday morning. I didn't want anyone to see me looking tear-stained and hopeless, and I couldn't bear the thought of having to talk to people or, even worse, of suddenly bursting into tears. But I didn't have much choice. I'd recently started working on a project that involved organising an exhibition at an art gallery in a town some distance from London, where I had to stay in a hotel for a couple of nights during the week. I was due to go back there that Monday morning, and had arranged a couple of important meetings for later in the day. I would have called in sick if it hadn't been for the fact that I knew the art specialist I was working with was on a tight schedule and was relying on me to help him get the job done on time.

So when the train pulled out of the station in London on Monday morning, I was on it, looking tired and strained, and trying not to think about everything I'd just lost or the fact that, in the space of just two very miserable days, almost every aspect of the life I thought I was going to have had changed.

The art specialist, Anthony, and I were staying at the same hotel and would often have something to eat together in the evenings. And although I tried to act normally that first Monday, he could obviously see that something was wrong. So eventually, when we got back to the hotel, I stopped saying, 'Yes, fine, thanks,' whenever he asked if I was all right, and told him that my boyfriend and I had split up. He was very nice, and seemed to understand that I didn't want to talk about it. Which meant that, for the next couple of days, I was able to throw myself into my work and not think about Jack or the future – until I was alone in my hotel room at night, when there was nothing to distract me from the misery that threatened to overwhelm me.

Somehow, I got through one day, then the next, then the rest of the week, then the weekend, which I spent alone again in the flat in London, snatching up my phone every time it rang in case it was Jack, calling to say he'd changed his mind; then not answering it because it wasn't ever him.

The first phase of the work I was doing with Anthony took a couple of months to complete, by which time I was getting better at pretending – to other people, at least – that everything was going to be all right, although I didn't actually believe that for a moment. While I was with Jack, I hadn't really thought about the future, except in general terms when we talked about getting married or about where we'd live and what sort of flat we'd buy when we had saved up enough money for a deposit. 'After Jack', I did try to imagine the future, but whenever I did I couldn't see anything in it for me at all, which was something I found incredibly frightening.

Looking back on it now, I realise that being dumped by Jack after we'd been together for seven years had shattered my already shaky self-confidence. At the time, however, I simply thought there was something wrong with me, that he had dumped me because I wasn't good enough, and that no other man would ever want me. So when Anthony and I got a bit drunk one evening at the hotel and ended up kissing, I was grateful to him for making me feel wanted again, even if it was only for a few minutes before embarrassment kicked in.

I went back to London the next day and didn't see Anthony again for a couple of weeks, when we met in another town to set up another exhibition. It was awkward at first, trying to pretend that we were purely work colleagues and that neither of us had any memory of having kissed. Then, one night, after we'd eaten our dinner together at the hotel and I'd gone back to my room, he knocked on my door and we ended up making love.

Pathetic as it might sound, it felt amazing to think that someone liked me enough to want to have sex with me, and that perhaps I did have something to offer after all. Anthony hadn't tried to hide the fact that he was married, so I had absolutely no excuse for getting involved with him. But when he told me that he hadn't ever had an affair before, that he loved me and simply couldn't help himself, the extraordinary thought began to form in my mind that maybe Jack didn't leave me because I'm unlovable and maybe my mother had been right and everything *was* going to be okay.

On the days when I was working with Anthony we maintained the same polite professional relationship we'd always had, then spent the nights together at whatever hotel we were staying at. So I don't think anyone guessed that there was something going on between us. If they did, they didn't ever say anything.

I can't remember what I thought at the time about what we were doing, or what I really felt about Anthony. Although he wasn't particularly charismatic or good-looking, he was a nice guy – if a man who cheats on his wife can ever really be called 'nice'. It's so stupid when I think about it now, and so naïve of me to have believed him when he told me some clichéd nonsense about his wife not understanding him. I imagine the truth was that she understood him only too well; and maybe his teenage son and daughter did too.

As Anthony was the one that was married, it could be said that his 'sin' was greater than mine. But I know that, in reality, I was as culpable as he was, because I knew that what I was doing was dishonest, which is why I didn't tell any of my friends about him, not even my flatmate Connie or my best friend, Sarah. All I can say in my defence – and I know it's a weak argument – is that I was so desperate to be loved and to feel valued that, at that particular moment in my life, I probably would have become involved with almost anyone who'd paid me any loving attention.

Anthony and I worked together on a few more projects after the first two, and spent pretty much every night together while we were away. He came to my flat in London sometimes too, on evenings during the week when Connie wasn't there, although he never stayed the night. He often told me he loved me, and I told myself that I'd fallen in love with him. Or maybe it wasn't simply a case of 'telling myself'; maybe I really did love him. I certainly thought I did at the time. But now I don't really know what I felt about anything.

We'd been seeing each other for a few weeks when something happened that should have rung alarm bells in my mind, but that completely failed to register with me as being peculiar in any way. I'd just been introduced to a researcher at an auction house where Anthony and I had been having some meetings, and while it was obvious that he already knew her, she was very frosty with him. When we were alone at the hotel later that evening, he made a point of telling me she was married and that they had an awkward relationship 'because I think she thought I once tried to make a move on her'. I didn't think any more about it until some time later, when I discovered he'd actually had numerous affairs before me, and that it was quite likely he was seeing other women while we were 'together'.

Sometimes, Anthony talked about his wife and about how things weren't working out between them. He didn't ever say he'd leave her, though, and I didn't ever ask him if he would. I don't know what I thought was going to happen in the long term. I can't really remember thinking about it at all. I was just happy to *have* someone – if you can call stealing time with someone else's husband 'having someone'.

You might think that having an affair with a married man would be complicated, whereas it was actually quite the opposite. The fact that he wasn't 'available' meant that we weren't a couple in the normal sense of the word, and as long as I didn't allow myself to feel too much, every aspect of our relationship was beyond my control – which meant that I didn't have to make any decisions, about the present or the future.

I'm the sort of person who likes to have people around me and things to do, so the weekends were very lonely. For years, Jack had been there every weekend and we'd done all the normal, reassuring things couples do. It seems like a very shallow thing to say in the circumstances, but even when I was seeing Anthony I think I was still clinging to the faint hope that Jack and I would get back together. I doubt whether it was ever a realistic hope, but it was kept alive to some extent by the fact that I was getting mixed messages from Jack, for example when he called in for a chat while I was at work one day, and when he sent me a card and a present for my thirtieth birthday.

One thing I've learned during the last few years is that you never really know what you'll do in a particular situation. So I can't say for certain that I'd have dropped Anthony if Jack had told me he'd changed his mind and wanted us to try to make a go of it. But I think I probably would have done so. Because even though I was in denial about it, I think I knew that my relationship with Anthony wasn't going anywhere. We didn't have to discuss it for me to realise that he wasn't going to leave his wife and children. In fact, I don't think that's what I wanted. Selfish as it sounds, the hours I spent with him were just a distraction from the loneliness and misery I felt when I was on my own.

By the time I was thirty years old I had a good job, money in the bank, and friends who were getting married, buying houses, having children and doing all the other things I'd thought I was going to do with Jack – which it now looked as though I might never do at all. It didn't matter how sternly I told myself, 'It's just a break-up. People go through far worse things in their lives. You'll get over it. You'll move on and meet someone else.' I didn't really believe it.

It felt as though Anthony was holding my head above water and that even though our relationship was wrong and probably didn't have any future, I might drown without him. So I told myself we were well suited and things would work out, and ignored what I suspected to be the truth – that we weren't and they wouldn't.

Then one Saturday morning, when I was alone in the flat, wondering what to do with myself for the rest of the weekend, Anthony phoned. His phone calls were usually to arrange our next meeting, or sometimes just to tell me he was missing me. On that occasion, however, he was at the airport, about to board a flight to Amsterdam, and the first thing he said was, 'We can't go on seeing each other.' And there it was again, the same feeling I'd had when Jack started to tell me it was all over between us, of wanting to freeze time so that whatever was going to happen next, didn't. But the clock kept ticking and Anthony kept talking.

It turned out that his daughter had found one of my texts on his phone, which said something like 'I miss you' or 'When will I see you again?' Apparently, she'd waited until her mother was out of the house before confronting him, and then had promised not to tell her as long as he swore never to see me again.

As I listened to what Anthony was telling me, I could feel my cheeks burning with distress for his daughter and, selfishly, for myself too. My family and friends had done everything they could think of to comfort and support me when Jack dumped me. So I knew they loved me and wanted me to be happy. But I was also aware that they would be appalled – my parents especially – if they knew I was having an affair with a married man. So I hadn't told even my closest friend. And now that I was being dumped again, I had no one to talk to, which I suppose was only what I deserved in the circumstances.

In hindsight, knowing what I know now about Anthony's many extramarital relationships, he might have been lying about the confrontation with his daughter and the promise he'd had to make to her. Perhaps it was what he told every woman he had an affair with when he was ready to move on. Saying 'I'm tired of you' or 'I've found someone else' would be likely to lead to tears and pleading, possibly even to acts of revenge. Whereas 'I still love you, but my daughter found your text message and I'm being forced to break it off for her sake' is rather more difficult to argue with. That didn't even cross my mind at the time, though, and I felt very guilty about my role in her distress.

So Anthony went to Amsterdam, and I spent the next few days feeling miserable and hating myself for lying to my mother every time she phoned and asked me what was wrong.

In fact, Anthony and I did start seeing each other again when he came back from Amsterdam. I can't remember exactly how it happened, just that, despite feeling ashamed and guilty, I did want to continue our relationship and was easily persuaded to sleep with him the next time we found ourselves staying at the same hotel. The only thing that really changed was that he insisted I mustn't ever contact him, which meant I had to wait for him to text or email me asking if my flatmate was out whenever he wanted to come to my flat for a couple of hours.

We'd been having an affair for about a year when he got a job that would take him out of London for weeks at a time. Even though we'd been seeing each other far less often during the last couple of months, we'd at least had some contact during working hours. Now, though, that was going to come to an end, and I couldn't imagine how our relationship could continue. If only I'd realised then that the best possible thing to do would be to draw a line under the mistake I'd made and end things with Anthony. By not doing so, I not only colluded with him in the lies he was telling his family, I also missed the opportunity to dispel the dark, destructive cloud that was about to cast its shadow over almost every aspect of my life.

And then I met Joe.

Chapter 3

Meeting Joe was like being offered the new beginning I didn't think I would ever have – or deserved. Suddenly, all the hurt and disappointment of the past didn't matter any more. Every day I spent with Joe seemed to be better than the day before. I had fallen head over heels in love with him, and what was even more extraordinary was that he seemed to feel the same way about me. We had only been seeing each other for about a week when he told me he loved me. 'I want to spend every minute of every day with you,' he said. And I wanted that too.

It all happened so quickly and was so intense that it must have looked crazy from the outside. I know some of my friends were a bit anxious on my behalf, particularly the ones who'd seen how hard I'd fallen when Jack left me. 'Do you think it might be a good idea to step back a bit?' one of them asked me, tentatively. But it didn't seem crazy at all from where I was standing. It felt completely right, and I was genuinely happy for the first time in years.

I'd told my mum about Joe during a phone call not long after we started going out. She didn't know about Anthony, of course, but she'd been worried about me ever since my bout of depression at university, and her concern had only been exacerbated by how upset I was after the split with Jack. So I thought she'd be really happy for me when I told her I'd found someone special. And she was – until she asked how old Joe was. 'That's a huge age gap,' she said, when I told her he was forty-four. 'It's only fourteen years,' I countered. 'And I'm thirty, not eighteen. I know what I want, Mum. And Joe does too.' But there seemed to be nothing I could say to ease her anxiety. So I didn't tell her when I moved in to live with him.

Ironically, perhaps, in view of Mum's reaction to the age difference between Joe and me, my dad is quite a bit older than she is, and of a generation of men who tend not to discuss personal matters and emotions. So I didn't talk to him about Joe at all.

I think it was because Mum was so concerned that she suddenly decided to come up to London for a flying visit. She said she just wanted to see me, but I knew that what she really wanted was an excuse to meet Joe and see for herself if her suspicions were correct and he really was the archetypal senior executive taking advantage of a younger colleague. Joe and I only met her briefly, for a coffee before she caught the train home again. But it was long enough for them to have a chat, and for Mum to decide that she liked him. Although she still had reservations about his age, she told me later, she no longer had any about his character.

To me, the difference in our ages was totally irrelevant and everything about our relationship seemed perfect. We were like the proverbial two peas in a pod, constantly surprised and delighted as we discovered still more things we agreed upon, views we shared, places we wanted to visit, books we loved or wanted to read … The list of our similarities seemed endless.

We drove to work together in the mornings, went out together in the evenings, slept together at night, and never once had an awkward moment or ran out of things to say to each other. I thought it was romantic when Joe told me, 'I don't *ever* want us to spend a single night apart.' Although I didn't think he meant it literally, it made me feel loved in a way I couldn't remember ever having felt before. And when he asked me to marry him, I didn't have to think about it for even a split second before I said yes, because spending the rest of my life with him seemed to be what I'd always been destined to do.

All the major decisions that would normally be made quite a long way down the line in any normal relationship had been made within two or three weeks of our first date at the bar. One of those decisions was that I would abandon my search for a flat, Joe would sell his house, and we would buy somewhere together. I always like to pay my own way, but although I was earning a good salary and had saved up almost £50,000 as a deposit on the flat I'd been intending to buy, Joe earned significantly more than I did and would be contributing considerably more to our joint house purchase and living costs. But, somehow, he made it seem as though we would be equal partners in everything we did.

I had a longstanding arrangement to go home to Devon for the weekend a couple of weeks after Mum's flying visit to London, and although I'd planned to go on my own, Joe said he was going to come with me. I wouldn't normally have taken a boyfriend home to meet my family in such a formal way so early in a new relationship, but I thought it was nice that Joe wanted to come. 'Why go all that way on the train when I can drive us there?' he said, when I told him I was quite happy to go on my own. 'I don't mind coming at all. And if we make a short detour on the way back on Sunday, we can have lunch with my mum. It'll be a family weekend.'

Even though I'd fallen for Joe and was happier with him than I'd ever been in my life before, I didn't really want to do the whole parent thing so soon. But somehow I ended up feeling as though it was what I'd wanted to do all along, and hadn't liked to suggest it because I thought it would be a pain for him.

We arrived at my parents' house late on the Friday evening, and the following morning Joe went out for a walk with my dad. Even when emotions aren't being discussed, Dad is a man of few words, and he and Joe had very little in common. But Joe is very good at talking to people about the things they're interested in, and when they came back from their walk together I could tell Dad liked him. In fact, everyone liked him. Joe's good at reading people and responding to them appropriately, so as well as talking to my dad about the things that interested him, he joked with my mum, and was friendly but respectful to my sisters and their boyfriends when they came for dinner on the Saturday evening. I always enjoyed spending time with my family, but that was a particularly good weekend and I was proud of the man I'd fallen in love with.

Joe and I left Devon on the Sunday morning and headed back towards London, stopping on the way to have lunch with his mother in a village near Bristol. That went well too, although Joe was very nervous about it beforehand. His relationship with his mother seemed ambivalent, and although the picture he painted of her was of a difficult woman, it was clear that she was also a very important figure in his life. So I was nervous too, especially after he told me she hadn't really liked his wife. But she was lovely, and when she apparently gave me her seal of approval during a phone call Joe made to her the next day, he was as happy as I had ever seen him.

A few days after our weekend in Devon, Joe suggested that we should go to Barcelona for a few days. I hadn't had a holiday for at least eighteen months – the last one would have been while I was going out with Jack – and Barcelona was high on both our lists of places we wanted to visit. So I was really looking forward to it, and I wasn't disappointed – by the city or by Joe.

When the time came, we walked around Barcelona until our feet ached, visited parks with extraordinary sculptures and art galleries that would have taken weeks to explore properly, sat in cafés, bars and restaurants talking about what we'd seen, hired a car and spent the day at the incredible Dalí Museum at Figueres, a couple of hours' drive north of the city, talked some more, walked some more, and had the most amazing sex I'd ever had.

Every time I looked at Joe, he was smiling, and I know I was too. Then one evening, when we were having dinner in a bar, he leaned across the table, kissed me and said, 'It's so easy being on holiday with you. I've had the most incredible time. I feel as though I've known you for years, not weeks. I adore you, Alice Keale.'

'I feel exactly the same,' I said. 'As though I'd known you all my life. In fact, I can't really remember what I felt about anything before I knew you.' And then we laughed about it later, when I pointed out to Joe that we'd become one of those nauseating, touchy-feely couples I used to roll my eyes at before I knew what it felt like to be in love and not to care what anyone else thinks.

Work seemed like something that existed in a parallel universe and I didn't want the holiday to end. I wanted to keep travelling with Joe, to visit all the places we'd always wanted to visit and do all the things we'd always wanted to do, safe inside our bubble of happiness. But although the holiday did have to end, we were still happy when we got home, because just *being* with Joe was an amazing experience.

In contrast to my dad's reticence when it came to talking about feelings and emotions, Joe was an open book. He told me about his relationship with his wife and how, towards the end of their marriage, the neighbours had phoned the police on several occasions when she lost her temper and started hurling furniture around their house. He mentioned another serious relationship too, which had lasted almost two years, until his girlfriend became pregnant and said she would only have the baby if he stayed with her, which he realised he no longer wanted to do. 'We were sitting in the car,' he told me, 'arguing, as we often did by that time, when she suddenly hit the window with her fist with such force that the glass shattered. In fact, it cut her hand so badly she had to go to A&E.'

He talked a bit about his family too, about how devastated his mother had been when his father left her for a younger woman, when Joe himself was just a little boy, and how he'd both pitied and despised her, because she was always crying and because, for reasons he didn't understand, he blamed her for the fact that he felt like the poor kid at his posh boarding school. He talked about his father's subsequent wives and girlfriends too, and about his half-sister, who was born when he was in his twenties and who he liked but rarely saw.

But although Joe was open about the subjects he chose to talk about, whenever I asked him any specific questions about his relationships he would say, 'This is about you, not me. I want to know everything about you, Alice Keale.' So I told him about my life too, which was uneventful by comparison. What I didn't tell him about was Anthony, I think because I wanted to be the person I saw reflected in Joe's eyes, and admitting that I'd had an affair with a married man with children – just like the woman who 'stole' his father – would have been like painting a jagged, ugly black line across a perfect picture.

We were in the living room in Joe's house one evening, sitting on the sofa, him at one end, me at the other, with my feet resting on his lap, when he said, 'I don't want us to have any secrets from each other. I want us to tell each other everything, to know that we can trust each other completely.'

'I do too,' I said, leaning forward as I spoke and putting my hand on his arm.

'So is there anything you haven't told me?' he asked. 'Any deep, dark secret you've been hiding from me that you want to make a clean breast of now?' He laughed as he said it, and I tried to laugh too, although all I managed was a weak smile.

Although Joe had already asked me to move in with him, I hadn't yet done so, and I was terrified that if he found out I wasn't as perfect as he seemed to believe I was, it would scare him off. But I knew he was right and that we needed to know we could trust each other implicitly, which meant I was going to have to tell him the one thing I didn't want him to know.

'There is one thing I haven't told you,' I said at last, ignoring the urgent voice in my head that was shouting, 'Don't do this.' Joe stopped massaging my feet, and when I dared to look up at him I saw that the smile had frozen on his face and there were anxious lines around his eyes. But it was too late to change my mind: if I didn't tell him now, he would only try to guess what the 'one thing' might be, and then, as the doubt grew inside him, it would eventually obliterate the love he felt for me.

'There is something you should know about me, Joe,' I persisted. 'I … I don't like talking about it. No one knows except my family and closest friends. I didn't tell Jack until we'd be going out for more than a year. But I want to be honest and open with you, the way I know you've been with me. So here goes.' I took a deep breath and pressed my hands against my stomach. 'I suffer from depression. I have done since I was eighteen. I take antidepressants every day – which, as you can see, work pretty well.' I made a small sound like a rueful laugh. 'It's stupid, I know,' I said quickly, suddenly wanting to keep talking so that I didn't have to hear whatever it was Joe was going to say. 'It isn't something anyone should feel ashamed of or be afraid to talk about. But I do worry about what people will think of me if they know, and about it scaring them away. About it scaring *you* away.'

I couldn't look at Joe while I was speaking. I didn't want to witness wary withdrawal replace the love that, until then, I'd seen in his eyes whenever he looked at me. So I thought the worst when he gently removed my feet from his lap. Then he edged along the sofa towards me, took my hands in his and said, 'I know, Alice. Or, at least, I guessed that it was something like that. But you're wrong to think it might scare me away. It doesn't bother me at all. In fact, it just makes me love you more.'

I didn't want to remove my hands from Joe's, so I let the tears drip slowly down my cheeks as I whispered, 'How did you know?'

'I saw you taking your meds one night,' he said. 'I just guessed.' His arms were around me now, pressing my body against his chest so that I could breathe in the warm smell of him I loved so much. 'But thank you, Alice.

Thank you for telling me and for trusting me. I know it was difficult for you. I hope you realise now that I mean it when I say that you can talk to me about *anything*.'

I felt like a child whose waning faith in fairies or Father Christmas had just been restored, but who could still barely believe the good news was true. I knew Joe really meant it, though: I *could* tell him anything and he would still look after me and protect me, because he loved me. But even then I ignored the voice in my head that asked, derisively, 'And what about Anthony?'

Although I didn't want people to know about the depression, I didn't ever try to pretend to myself that it wasn't real. I was just wary of telling people about it because I didn't know what they'd think, or if they'd treat me differently when they knew. Having it didn't make me feel guilty or ashamed, though, which is the way I'd always felt about my relationship with Anthony, even before I met Joe.

Sitting with Joe's arms around me made me feel safe and loved. So should I tell him about Anthony, and that he was still in touch with me? The knowledge of my depression hadn't fazed him at all. Would he respond in the same way to the news that I'd had an affair with a married man who I still hadn't told, categorically, that I was in love with someone else and it was over? Or would that be testing his love for me by pushing my luck one huge step too far?

In the end, I decided not to tell Joe my shameful secret. Instead, I would tell Anthony, once and for all, that I didn't want to see him or have any contact with him any more.

After I started seeing Joe, I had stopped contacting Anthony, who must have realised after a few days that something was going on and sent me an email asking, 'Are you pulling away?' I should have been honest with him then and said 'Yes'. How difficult would it have been to answer his email with just that one word, and to draw a line under the most shameful thing I had ever done in my life? Instead, I denied it.

I don't know if not breaking things off with Anthony was purely cowardice on my part, because I thought ours was the only extramarital affair he'd ever had and couldn't bring myself to hurt him when I believed he'd risked everything by falling in love with me. It sounds stupid when I actually say it like that, and I don't think I ever did think it through clearly in those terms. I just didn't want to compound one mistake with another by hurting him. Perhaps, even more selfishly, I was also afraid of not having a safety net if things didn't work out with Joe – although I certainly didn't think that consciously at the time.

The fact is, though, that whatever reason I thought I had for not telling Anthony it was all over between us, there was no excuse for telling him I missed him. And now my cowardice and duplicity were coming back to haunt me. What was worse, though, was that one day, after I'd told Joe about my depression, I agreed to meet Anthony for lunch. I didn't want to go. I felt anxious and slightly panicky just thinking about it. But I didn't know what else to do when he asked me. And then there we were, sitting facing each other across a table in a café, Anthony crying and refusing to look at me, while I sat staring at my uneaten food and wondering why on earth I had come.

'I'm sorry,' I told him again, 'but I love Joe. What do you expect me to do, Anthony? We haven't seen each other for weeks. You're married. You've got a family, people to go home to every day. And now I've got someone who cares about me too. Can't you be happy for me?'

'Just don't say anything else.' Anthony's face was contorted by distress. 'I can't believe that you went away with this man. I don't think I can cope with this. I don't want to hear any more.' His distress had turned to anger as he spoke and he almost spat the last words at me. But I was angry too. It wasn't fair of him to make me feel so guilty, after all the lonely hours I'd spent during the last few months, waiting and wondering if he was going to call me, not being able to text him in case his daughter looked at his phone again and told his wife that he'd been seeing someone else. He had always said that our relationship couldn't go anywhere, that he would never leave his wife and children. He'd been honest about that at least. And I'd accepted it, because having part of someone seemed better than having no one at all.

As we sat there, silently blaming each other for our pain, I suddenly knew that I didn't love Anthony and hadn't ever really loved him, whatever I might have told myself. So why had I sent him emails telling him that I did? Why, even after I started seeing Joe, had I typed the words, 'Yes, I *do* love you, Anthony. No one could ever equal you.'

I was telling the truth now, though. Finally, I was facing the reality of what I'd done. I didn't know why I'd done it. But I did know that nothing could ever remove the stain my amoral actions had imprinted so irrevocably on the story of my life. I already hated the fact that I'd been someone's mistress and a cheat, and now I felt terrible because my happiness was hurting Anthony. What I had done had been an aberration: the real Alice Keale wasn't an amoral person; she was the person who loved Joe, openly and honestly. But Anthony knew me well enough to know that I was weak too, and that by manipulating my emotions he would make it difficult for me to cut the tenuous bond that existed between us and walk away.

Suddenly, I felt suffocated, and when Anthony stood up, having barely touched his food, I stood up too, and followed him out of the café. I'd always liked the fact that he was much taller than me, but when he stopped on the pavement outside and I looked up into his face I wondered what else I'd ever really liked about him, and why I'd allowed myself to become involved with a man who didn't even come close to Joe, and wouldn't have done so even if he hadn't had a wife and family. It was hard to believe I'd been so unhappy, and so desperate for someone to want me, that I'd compromised my own integrity, risked breaking up another woman's marriage, and convinced myself I loved him.

'I'm sorry,' I said again. 'I've got to get back to work.' Then I turned and walked away.

As soon as I was back in the office, I wrote an email to Anthony, unequivocal this time, telling him it really was over, that I didn't love him and that I was tired of feeling guilty. 'I'm happy with Joe,' I wrote. 'It took finding someone I really love to make me realise that our affair always was a mistake. I'm tired of lying and hiding our relationship. I want my life to be simple and uncomplicated again.'

As I typed, I felt a sense of relief flood over me. Then, just as I was about to press 'Send', an email appeared in my Inbox and I made the huge mistake of opening it first. By the time I'd read just the first two sentences, relief had been replaced by guilt again, because I believed that I was to blame for the pain Anthony was suffering. The sense I'd had since walking away from Anthony outside the café, of being strong and empowered by Joe's love, simply evaporated and I knew I was too weak to cut him out of my life completely. Not because I wanted to have any contact with him, but because I felt that, having disrupted his life the way I believed I had done, it was my duty not to be the cause of distress.

So instead of sending my sensible, honest email, I agreed to meet Anthony for a drink after work a few days later, to celebrate his birthday. Then I tried to forget about him, which wasn't difficult when I was with Joe.

One of the many things I liked so much about Joe was the fact that he was never afraid to show his feelings. I had a friend at university who went out with a guy who became almost hysterical if she tried to hold his hand in public. She left him eventually – partly because she couldn't understand his reluctance to make what she saw as a statement to other people that they were a couple – and I can remember how bemused she was when he was upset, and how someone explained to her that some people just find it difficult to express their feelings. Well, Joe was the complete opposite of my friend's erstwhile boyfriend, and he would often stop in the street to kiss me or tell me he loved me.

Another thing I liked about Joe was being driven by him. It's such a simple thing, but it made me feel safe and relaxed to know that I didn't have to do anything at all except sit beside him while he got us from wherever we were to wherever we were going. He liked to play music, loudly, in his car, and we were driving back from a restaurant one evening, singing along to his favourite song, when he suddenly stopped in the middle of the road.

'What's wrong?' I asked him, sliding my feet back into the shoes I'd kicked off as soon as I'd sunk into my seat. 'What is it, Joe? Are you okay?'

'I'm fine,' he told me, smiling as he always did. 'In fact, I'm more than fine. I just wanted to tell you that I love you.' Then he undid his seat belt, opened the car door and started to get out.

'What are you doing?' I asked him, laughing despite my bemusement. 'Where are you going, Joe? What if a car comes up behind us?'

'It's a residential street and almost midnight,' he said. 'No one will come up behind us. And if they do, they'll understand when I explain that I *had* to stop because I was so full of love for my perfect girlfriend that I wanted to run with her to the top of that hill and tell the world how wonderful she is.' As he spoke, he pointed to a grassy slope in the park where we often sat and read newspapers at the weekends. Then he ran around the car, opened my door with a flourish, got down on one knee on the cold tarmac and said, in mock solemnity, 'I adore you, Alice Keale. I want to spend the rest of my life with you.'

We were both laughing as he took my hand and we ran together to the top of the hill, where he wrapped me in his coat, put his arms around me, whispered, 'I love you so much, Alice,' and kissed me.

It was just one of Joe's many spontaneous and romantic gestures. There were several occasions while we were on holiday in Barcelona when we found ourselves in some particularly beautiful spot and he got down on one knee and declared his undying love for me. He did it in London too, suddenly shouting 'I love you, Alice Keale' while we were buying food in the supermarket – which amused the other shoppers and made me blush. He left notes for me on the door of the fridge, had flowers delivered to my desk while I was at work, and ran out of the house in the middle of the night to buy chocolates at the 24-hour off-licence because I'd said, jokingly, that I wanted some.

It probably all sounds ridiculously sentimental to anyone else, the sort of over-the-top behaviour that isn't normally indulged in by anyone beyond their teens. But I can't describe the effect it had on me at the time. No one had *ever* shown me love like that before. No one had ever made me feel so special or so wanted. And as well as being in love with Joe, I think I was in love with that feeling too. I suppose that's why I didn't stop to wonder if it might all be too good to be true.

Chapter 4

I was thirty years old, I had a well-paid job that I loved, I'd saved up enough money to put down a deposit on a flat in London and, for the first time in my life, I had someone who was both willing and able to share with me whatever the future would bring. Why would anyone in their right mind risk throwing all that away and hurting the man they loved? In my case, the answer seems to have been because I was too afraid to say 'It's over' to a man whose daughter probably hadn't found a text on his phone and threatened to tell her mother – his wife – about me, who turned out to have had a string of girlfriends before me, and who went on to have many more when I had gone.

I don't know why I did any of it: why I got involved with Anthony in the first place, why I didn't break things off with him as soon as I met Joe, or why I lied to the man I truly believed was the one person who could, and would, make me happy and give me the future I'd begun to think I would never have.

When I'd agreed to have a drink with Anthony on his birthday, I think I had some misguided idea that if I told Joe most of the truth – that it was a friend's birthday (true) and that several of us (not true) were meeting at the bar I was actually going to – it wouldn't be as bad as lying about all of it. It was a stupid idea and a banal delusion to think that lying to Joe about anything to avoid upsetting Anthony would end any other way than in tears.

Quite late one Friday evening, a few days before Anthony's birthday, he sent me a text. Joe was already in bed, and I was in the bathroom when the phone I'd left on the bedside table must have pinged. Although Anthony's name would have come up on the screen, Joe didn't say anything about it until we were getting ready to go out for coffee the next morning, when he suddenly said, 'I'm probably just being silly, but who's Anthony?'

That's the trouble with telling a lie: you think, 'It'll just be this one' – but it never is. Because after you've told one lie, there comes a time when you have to decide whether to come clean and admit it, or whether to tell another to hide the first one. It's hard to choose the first option, especially when it involves having to admit to someone whose opinion you value that you haven't been honest with them. But if you choose the second, you become like an inept spider, spinning a web around yourself that will eventually tangle and trap you in its silken threads. What's even worse about the second option, however, is that the more lies you tell, the more you end up despising yourself, and then you start to doubt whether the person you love could ever really love someone like you.

I didn't know that then, of course. So I chose option two and told Joe, 'Oh, he's just a colleague. He's going to be at this birthday thing next week.' Then I laughed and added, 'I'm not interested in him, if that's what you were thinking. He's a married man, with children.'

I hated myself for the glibness of my deceit. But at least I seemed to have allayed any latent suspicions Joe might have had – or so I thought, until I found out later that he'd been planning to come to the bar and witness the truth for himself.

A few days before Anthony sent me that text, Joe had asked me for the pass code for my phone. 'I want us to be able to read each other's emails and texts and to merge our contacts,' he told me, which some people might not have wanted to do, but which seemed like a nice thing to me. I don't know why I deluded myself into believing I had nothing to hide. Perhaps all my attention was focused on fulfilling my wish to become part of something. Maybe that was also the reason why I didn't really register the fact that, although I gave Joe my pass code and contacts, he didn't actually give me his.

It was a Tuesday morning a couple of days before Anthony's birthday and I was making coffee in the kitchen before work when I thought I heard Joe calling me. 'Do you want me?' I called back. 'Joe? I'm in the kitchen.' When he didn't answer, I flicked the switch on the espresso machine and then snatched the pan of spitting milk off the hob, turning my head away as the sickly smell filled my nostrils and inhaling the far more pleasant aroma of strong coffee.

At that moment, a drop of rain hit the skylight above my head and I looked up at the grey clouds that had been gathering slowly all morning. It was the time of year I liked least: late autumn, I suppose you'd call it, although it already felt like winter. I hated the short winter days, when the sun sometimes seemed barely to have climbed above the horizon before it started sinking again, sucking all the light and energy out of the afternoon until all I wanted to do was go home and close the door.

I knew I wasn't the only one who found the winter a bit depressing, or whose footsteps lightened and quickened when the spring came again. But on that particular day the rain and darkness of the morning didn't bother me at all. It was five weeks since Joe and I had sat together in a bar for the first time and, for once, I was looking forward to the impending winter, when we would start putting in motion the plans we had made, to sell Joe's house and look for one to buy together, before we got married in the spring.

I took a spoon out of the drawer and scooped up the skin that had formed on the milk in the pan, then tried to rinse it off under the tap, which never worked, but was something I did every time before dropping the spoon into the sink. I'd just put a cup on the espresso machine when I thought I heard Joe call my name again. 'Did you say something?' I called back, then took a step towards the kitchen door and listened. But the house was silent.

'Damn,' I said aloud, realising that I hadn't positioned the cup correctly on the machine and some of the coffee had dripped down the outer surface of the white china and formed a small, dark pool on the worktop.

'You lied to me!' I was so startled by Joe's voice that I yelped as I spun round and saw him standing in the open doorway of the kitchen. He was holding something in his hand, but it was the look on his face that made me gasp again. His lips formed a thin line – of pain or distress, I couldn't tell which – and there was anger in his eyes where I had only ever seen love and warmth.

My first thought was that he was in physical pain, and I took a step towards him as I asked, 'What is it? What's happened?' Then I froze when he turned his head away from me as if in disgust.

'I said, you lied to me.' Joe repeated the words slowly. 'About Anthony. So tell me, Alice, who is Anthony really, this married man who's just a colleague?'

And there it was – the lie, filling the space between us like something smashed and toxic.

My heart was racing and all I could think was, 'What have I done? How could I have been so stupid?' Suddenly, I knew with absolute certainty that only a fool, or someone with nothing to lose, would have chosen option two. I should have told Joe about Anthony when I had the chance. I should have explained to him how ashamed I was of getting involved with a married man, but that, until the first magical evening we had spent together five weeks ago, I had truly believed I might never get over the break-up with Jack, that no one would ever want me again, and that crushing depression would eventually take over my life and destroy any chance I might have had of finding love and happiness.

If I had done that – and if I'd had the courage to tell Anthony it was over – instead of compounding one lie with another, Joe *might* have understood and forgiven me. At least there would have been a chance, however slim, that he'd have valued my honesty in telling him more than he'd have despised me for having a deceitful affair with a married man. But now I risked losing him. And if I lost Joe, I'd lose everything that mattered to me. Worse still was the knowledge that I had hurt the one man I truly loved.

Why hadn't I thought about all that before, when there was still a chance to tell the truth voluntarily? Nothing good could come out of it now, and as the terrible permutations ran through my head, I found myself struggling to breathe. There was still one certainty, though: I *couldn't* lose Joe. And as my mind began to clear, I realised that, having chosen option two, I was stuck with it, and I was going to have to lie to Joe again.

'Joe …' I reached out my hand and took another step towards him, but he turned and ran out of the kitchen and down the stairs. As I ran after him, stumbling and only just managing to grab the banister in time to save myself from falling, I saw him snatch up my iPhone from the hall table.

'Give it to me,' I pleaded with him. 'Please, Joe, don't …' Grasping his hand, I tried to prise his fingers apart so that he would release the phone. But he was much stronger than me and so upset that he barely seemed to be aware that I was touching him. And while we stood there in the hallway of his house, facing what, for me, might be the worst disaster of my life, I was thinking about all the emails I'd sent Anthony, all the stupid, cowardly lies I'd told him during the last six weeks.

I didn't know what Joe had already seen, but I knew with desperate, gut-clenching certainty that he mustn't read those emails. It didn't matter that what I said in them wasn't true. By lying to Anthony, I had betrayed Joe too. Like Judas. The two words were still echoing in my head when Joe suddenly pushed past me and ran back up the stairs and into the bathroom, slamming and bolting the door before I'd even turned and followed him.

'Open the door, please, Joe.' I pressed my forehead against it as I spoke. 'Let me explain. Please, Joe. Just give me my phone and I can explain it all to you. It isn't what it seems.' I was crying now, but Joe didn't answer. 'If you don't open the door, I'll take all my pills and kill myself,' I sobbed. I don't know what made me say it. I don't think I'd have done it. So perhaps, on some subconscious level, I just wanted proof that he still cared enough about me to want to stop me. And he did open the door. But when I reached out my hand and tried to grab his arm, he almost flung me against the wall as he ran past me into the kitchen, snatched an orange from the fruit bowl and threw it at me, while I stood in the doorway, shaking with anguish and despair.

'I should never have trusted you,' he shouted at me. 'I haven't ever told anyone some of the things I've told you. The first time in my life I trust someone and open up to them, and look what happens.' His self-deprecating laugh was almost worse than his anger, which returned almost immediately as he pointed to the open door of the living room and shouted, 'Right there on the sofa. We were sitting right there when we talked about trust for the first time. No secrets, that's what we agreed. I *asked* you, Alice: is there anything else you want to tell me? And you said no. I was so happy. And now you've ruined everything. I don't understand. Explain it to me, Alice. How could you do this to me?'

Then, suddenly, his anger seemed to burst like a bubble, leaving him limp and depleted. Sinking into a chair, he put his head in his hands and began to cry. I was sobbing too, but I stayed where I was in the doorway, not daring to move towards him or try to touch him, because I knew that it was my lies and deceit that had broken him.

When Joe eventually raised his head again, the expression on his face was like that of a vulnerable little boy who's been overwhelmed by emotions he doesn't understand and can't control. I did take a step towards him then. I wanted to wrap my arms around him, to do *something* to smooth away the hurt and make him happy again. But I found that I couldn't touch him, because I knew *I* had caused the pain he was suffering. I had taken the trust of a good man and snapped it with my bare hands. And for what? Perhaps it would have been understandable – although no less despicable – if I *had* loved Anthony, then or ever. But when faced with a choice between hurting a man I didn't love and breaking the trust of a man I adored, I'd chosen – for some inexplicable, incomprehensible reason – to do the one thing that would hurt both of us more than we had ever been hurt in our lives before.

I knew then that I couldn't stop Joe from reading the emails I'd sent Anthony. And when he had read them he would know the truth – not that I loved Anthony, which I didn't, but that I was a deceitful liar; and then he would leave me.

'How did I become this person?' I asked myself. I wasn't brought up to tell lies. It was so out of character, so unlike the real me. Making the drunken decision to get involved with Anthony that first night in the hotel had been like crossing a line between honesty and deceit. Once I'd crossed it, lying seemed to have become easier – almost imperative, I'd allowed myself to believe. Now Joe hated me because I'd broken his heart; but not as much as I hated myself.

I hadn't seen Anthony since that miserable lunchtime we'd spent together, when I told him I loved Joe and broke things off with him, before later relenting and agreeing to meet him on his birthday. And although I'd deleted all the texts we'd exchanged, there were still emails for Joe to read, full of the false words I'd written to Anthony. So I begged him again to give me my phone and let me delete them, but he refused.

Joe's reaction to what I now think of as 'the discovery' was dramatic. He was very angry, distraught and heart-broken. But although he shouted and screamed at me, he wasn't violent. He didn't tell me to leave and then throw my clothes out on to the street after me, as he might have done. He didn't even say he needed some time alone so he could think. In fact, he didn't seem to want me to go. And as I was desperate to cling on to any part of what we'd had, in the hope of somehow being able to make amends, I called in sick at work that morning and stayed.

For the rest of that day, Joe trawled through my emails and bombarded me with questions. I knew Joe despised me for being dishonest; I didn't want him to hate me even more for being sexually amoral too. So I continued to deny that the relationship I'd had with Anthony had ever been sexual. Then Joe found the emails that proved otherwise and I realised, too late, that I'd made everything even worse than it might otherwise have been, because now he knew he couldn't believe anything I said about anything.

The questioning continued without a break throughout the entire day. Bizarrely, perhaps, we went to a local bistro for lunch, although we barely touched our food, in Joe's case because the only time he stopped asking me questions was when he was dry retching.

We hardly slept that night either. Joe wanted to know everything about my affair with Anthony, where and when we had slept, what I'd been wearing on each occasion, what I'd said to him and what he'd said to me, every tiny detail about the hotel room … Answering his endless stream of questions was exhausting and humiliating. But if that's what it was going to take to make Joe understand why I'd lied, it was worth it.

I still wonder sometimes what I would have done that day – the day of the discovery – if I'd known what lay ahead.

I didn't leave Joe's flat that day because I was afraid that, if I did, everything would be over between us forever, and because Joe didn't ask me to go. Instead, the barrage of questions continued, with Joe asking them in a voice that was sometimes angry, sometimes cold, and me answering them as best I could, first with more lies, then by telling him as much as I dared of the truth. I knew that, because of what he'd discovered, Joe had changed his opinion of me completely, and it felt as though everything that had been perfect was irrevocably spoiled and horrible.

'How could you get involved with a married man?' he kept asking me, and every time he said it I thought about what his dad had done when Joe was a little boy and how badly it had affected him at the time and – I realise now – ever since. 'What you did is abhorrent,' Joe said. And there really wasn't anything I could do but agree.

As well as being distraught about what I'd done to Joe, I was afraid of my mother finding out about my affair with Anthony, because I knew she would be equally appalled. And I was worried about the negative impact I knew the situation with Joe would have on our relationship at work too, although that was one of my lesser anxieties at the time.

If You Love Me

In the end, neither of us went to work for the rest of the week. I don't know what excuse Joe gave. He was in quite a senior position, so I don't suppose anyone would have questioned whatever he said. The thought of having to go in to work filled me with dread at the time, but in fact staying at home with Joe turned out to be even worse. For the rest of that week Joe never stopped questioning me except when we were asleep, between the hours of about 4 and maybe 7 or 8 a.m., when he started again, sometimes before my eyes were even open.

When I finally admitted that my relationship with Anthony had been sexual, Joe demanded to know every tiny detail of every insignificant aspect of every single occasion when we had been together. 'It was before you and I met,' I told him. 'I lied to you about Anthony because I didn't want to lose you. He doesn't matter to me, Joe. My affair with him was a terrible mistake. So how can it possibly make any difference, or help in any way, for you to know what colour top I was wearing the first night we had sex or what sort of cover there was on the bed in the hotel? Please, Joe. None of this is relevant to *us*.'

'You made it relevant to us when you lied to me,' was all he said, coldly. And I suppose he was right. But the same explanation surely didn't apply to every other relationship I'd ever had, the details of which Joe now also wanted to know. 'And did you cheat on them too?' he asked me, when I told him about Jack – who he already knew about – and another boyfriend I'd had at university.

'Of course I didn't,' I said. 'And I didn't cheat on *you*, Joe. I know I lied to you, but only because I was ashamed of what I'd done. But I didn't sleep with Anthony after I met you. You *know* that's true, Joe. I wouldn't have wanted to, because I love you.' And it *was* true. In fact, the only time I'd even seen Anthony since I'd met Joe had been that lunch we'd had together when I'd told him that our relationship was over.

I was so weary by the end of the second day that I would have done almost anything to make the questioning stop. Anything except give up on my relationship with Joe and walk away. There had to be some way to fix what I'd broken, and if Joe thought the solution lay in the questions he was asking me, I had no alternative but to answer them, however many times he repeated them and however trivial or unrelated to anything that mattered they appeared to be.

By the weekend, Joe was sometimes asking me the same questions over and over again for hours on end. Then he started making me write accounts of what had happened, and after he'd read them he asked me more questions.

'What were you wearing the first time with him?'

'What colour were your jeans?'

'What top were you wearing?'

'I thought you said the room was hot. If that's true, why would you be wearing a top like that?'

It was like a form of torture and I wanted to scream at him to stop. The first time I described an article of clothing I'd been wearing on a particular occasion, Joe made me fetch it from the wardrobe, cut it up and put it in the bin. But by the time I'd said the same thing over and over again, I became so exhausted and confused that I began to doubt myself. Was I really wearing the top I'd said I was wearing? I'd been certain about it a hundred questions earlier; but now I wasn't so sure. Perhaps I had made a mistake. What top did I tell him it was? If I say something different the next time he asks me, he'll think I've deliberately lied – for some reason I couldn't even begin to imagine.

I knew that Joe was deeply wounded to discover that the woman he apparently thought was perfect had been sending emails to another man. But the more hours he kept me awake, the more questions he asked and then asked again, the less able I became to think logically.

Because I felt guilty about having hurt him, I wrote the accounts he told me to write and answered his never-ending questions. Of course I had another option – I could have opened the front door and walked out of his house that first day, or the day after that, or on any of the days that followed. But I didn't believe at the time that I had a choice. I thought that if I could manage to stick with it just a little bit longer, Joe would eventually say, 'I understand now. I believe you. What you did has caused me enormous distress and has shaken my trust in you. But I think we're going to be all right. I think we can get back to where we were, or at least somewhere close to it, now that I know the truth about your relationship with this married man and why you didn't tell me about it.'

I suppose I felt the same way gamblers must feel: if I stop now, everything I've already invested will be lost; whereas if I keep going, I can make it all right again, and have the man I love with all my heart back with me. So I sat there in Joe's house for hour after miserable hour, answering and re-answering his questions, and writing and re-writing detailed accounts of irrelevant incidents.

It was a couple of days after the discovery when Joe told me he was going to phone my mother, and although I begged him not to, he was determined. 'She needs to know what you've done,' he told me, and I felt so guilty about it that I couldn't really argue with him. So he put the phone on speaker and I sat beside him on the bed, with my heart racing, as he said, in a calm, quiet voice, 'Mrs Keale? Barbara? It's Joe. I don't know how you tell this, but your daughter has had an affair with a married man.'

At first, Mum obviously didn't understand what he was saying, which was reasonable enough in the circumstances. But Joe explained what had happened and told her, 'I love Alice and I want our relationship to work. But she's really betrayed and hurt me.' And then my mother confirmed everything he'd already made me believe about myself by saying, 'This is awful, Joe. I simply can't believe it. I'm *so* sorry about my daughter.'

My mother isn't particularly religious, but she is quite puritanical in many ways and I knew she'd be shocked by what Joe told her. To be fair, even the least censorious person would probably have shared her opinion about the amorality of having an affair with a married man – I would have done so myself a couple of years earlier. But the fact that she was so appalled by what I'd done and sided so unequivocally with Joe felt to me as though she was also endorsing his behaviour towards me and that he was right to be reacting the way he was.

I didn't say anything during that phone call and I don't know if Mum could hear me crying. She didn't speak to me, though, or even ask to do so, which was hurtful in one respect, because it didn't even seem to cross her mind that what Joe was telling her might not be true, but was also a relief, because I didn't want to talk to her. By the time Joe said goodbye to her I was convinced that what I'd done was on a par with the worst possible type of crime imaginable. And it *was* a bad thing, I know that. It's certainly something I'm still ashamed of. But maybe it was more stupid and selfish than evil. I wouldn't expect Anthony's wife and children ever to forgive me if they knew. But my own mother …? Her disgust and reprobation simply reinforced what Joe was already telling me, which was that what I had done was terribly wrong.

I don't blame my mum for her reaction – I'm certainly not in any position to criticise her for it. It was just unfortunate that it made me feel as though I couldn't go home, which meant that I wouldn't have had anywhere to go if I *had* tried to walk away from Joe.

My sisters were shocked too, when they found out. But they were more forgiving than my mother had been. Instead of condemning me out of hand, their attitude was that it was a stupid thing to have done, not good for anyone involved, but so out of character for me that I must have been even more upset than they'd realised about the split with Jack.

Joe insisted on my telling my best friend Sarah too. She was abroad on holiday at the time, but she sent me a text as soon as she received mine, asking, 'Are you okay? It's not the end of the world, you know!' Clearly, it wasn't the response Joe had hoped for, and when he took the phone out of my hand and read Sarah's text, he said it proved what he already suspected – that I'd surrounded myself with friends who were as morally depraved as I was and with whom it really would be better for me not to have any further contact.

I didn't realise it then, of course, but having made me despise myself for what I'd done, Joe was moving on to the next step – isolating me from all the people who loved me and who I cared about.

Chapter 5

Within the space of just a few weeks Joe had become the centre of my emotional life. He played a pivotal role in my working life too, and I knew that if we broke up he would make things very difficult for me. After his phone conversation with my mother, I couldn't bear the thought of going home to face her disapproval and disappointment. And as I was also too ashamed to face my friends, so didn't feel that I had anywhere else to go, I was trapped.

It was the day after Joe phoned my mum that I suggested talking to a therapist. The vehemence of his reaction to the discovery frightened me, and I knew we weren't going to be able to deal on our own with the can of vicious worms we'd inadvertently opened. I'd been seeing a counsellor called Paula fairly regularly for some time, for cognitive behavioural therapy (CBT) and just to have someone to talk to, having been referred to her by my psychiatrist. I saw her privately every six months or so, as a failsafe – and I always felt better after the sessions I had with her. Now, I needed to talk to her more urgently than I'd ever done before.

I felt anxious about suggesting to Joe that we should see Paula together, and I was surprised when he agreed. I wouldn't normally have rung her on a Sunday, but I was desperate, and almost cried with relief when she answered the phone. I was sitting on the bedroom floor in my underwear when I made the call, and Joe was watching me from the bed, his back resting against the headboard as he looked at me over the top of some glasses I hadn't ever seen him wear before. He hated glasses, he'd once told me. 'They make me look too serious.' But maybe his tears had washed out the contact lenses he usually wore, or maybe his eyes were as tired as mine were and they were sore. As I glanced up at him, I suddenly remembered that just a few days earlier, when we were sitting together in his bed, he'd said to me, 'Let's promise never to have a cross word,' and I'd laughed and promised, because anything had seemed possible with Joe then.

'So, Alice,' he said now, when I finished my phone call with Paula, 'please tell me she can fit us in. I don't think I can get through another day like this.'

'She said she'd see us at three,' I told him. 'I'm sure she'll be able to help us, Joe.' I knew someone had to. We'd barely slept or eaten for the last five days. When Joe wasn't screaming at me, he was sobbing or dry retching, bending almost double as he tried to expel the vomit that was either imaginary or got stuck in his throat. He looked terrible – as I know I did too – and it was all my fault. I knew, in some abstract way, that I deserved to be punished for what I'd done. But as each exhausting, horrible day merged into the next one, I couldn't help wondering whether there was any useful purpose to be served for either of us by the punishment Joe was so relentlessly inflicting on me.

Since the moment of the discovery, he hadn't once asked me to leave, although, long before that Sunday, I'd begun to wish he would. Surely it would be better for him to have some time on his own, I thought, so that he could sleep and eat while he tried to work things through in his mind. But despite the huge stress my presence caused him, he seemed to want me to stay.

Joe did most of the talking during our session with Paula on that Sunday afternoon. I was so worn down by all the questioning and lack of sleep, I couldn't think clearly enough to be able to say anything constructive. So for more than three hours I sat beside him on the couch where I'd sat on my own many times before and, while he ranted and raved, I looked out of the high sash window at the steadily darkening buildings across the road, and cried.

Although Paula remained professional and impartial throughout, I could tell by the red blotches that appeared on her neck and chest, and by the set of her lower jaw when she clenched her teeth, that she was becoming increasingly frustrated and, eventually, wanted us to go.

'I can see that you're very upset,' she said to Joe, interrupting him as he asked the same question he'd asked maybe twenty times since he'd sat down. 'But do you think it's possible that your reaction might be a bit extreme? I wonder if we could try and …'

Now it was Joe's turn to interrupt, although I don't know if he'd even heard what she said. 'Why did she do it?' he asked yet again. 'Why did she lie? How could she have had an affair with a married man? What sort of amoral person does that?'

Suddenly, I knew what children who have tantrums must feel like and why they throw themselves down on the floor, kicking and screaming and drumming with their fists. I wanted to do that now, to launch myself on to the neat white rug and howl like a child. In fact, I was too preoccupied by the sensation of being unable to breathe to realise immediately that the sound I could hear – like an animal in pain – was coming from me. It even made Joe stop talking for a moment. Then I threw my arms around his neck, buried my face in the soft warmth of his jumper, and kept repeating, 'I'm sorry. I'm so sorry for what I did. But *please* stop. I love you, Joe. I don't want to lose you. I'll do anything to try to move past this. But I can't take much more. Please, *please*, stop.'

'You can see how sorry she is, Joe.' Paula had to raise her voice to be heard above the sound of my sobs. 'You've only been dating for about a month. I've known Alice for a year, and I know that she's a good person. She made a mistake. She admits that and she's genuinely sorry. She wants to stay with you, Joe, and you say that you love her and want to stay with her, too. So let's try to work towards moving past this and rebuilding your relationship.'

Everything Paula said, in her calm, measured tones, was indisputably rational and logical. Joe would see that, I was sure, because he was normally rational and logical too. All he needed was enough time to clear his head and absorb the things she'd said. So I sat silently beside him in the car on the way back to his house, wishing I was the woman I could see walking her dog on the damp pavement, or the one holding hands with a man and laughing.

Suddenly, there was a sound of screeching brakes and my head jerked sideways, then slammed against the glass on which I'd been resting it. As I turned to look at Joe, I remember thinking that I was so tired I was barely aware of the pain.

'She didn't know what she was talking about,' Joe snapped at me, his eyes almost glowing with indignation and resentment. 'I don't agree with a single thing she said. I think we should find a new therapist, one that deals with couples. Why did you do it, Alice? Why did you betray my trust? Why did you pretend to be an honest person when really you're nothing more than an amoral whore? Why, Alice? You've done this to me, and now I need you to answer my questions.'

'Four hours,' I thought. 'We sat in that room for almost four hours, and it hasn't helped Joe at all. Four hours with a therapist bought me just five minutes without any questions.' They were questions to which I had no answers. What I'd done couldn't be explained or excused. So what could I say?

I thought Joe had agreed to see the therapist with me because he wanted to find a reason to forgive me, so that we could work things out and get back to the way we had been – two soul mates who'd had the immense good fortune to find each other. But it was almost as if he had no intention of trying to get past what had happened and that he'd only gone with me because he thought my therapist would listen to what he said and then tell me he was right, that what I'd done *was* unforgivable, and explicable only as the act of someone who was not in their right mind.

A couple of days later I phoned my psychiatrist – the one who'd originally referred me to Paula – and asked her to recommend someone else. 'Paula told me about the session you had with her on Sunday,' the psychiatrist said. 'Are you all right, Alice? It sounds as though your boyfriend's reaction is very extreme.' Even then I didn't hear the voice of reason in my head that *must* have been saying, 'Walk away from him. Protect yourself before it's too late.' So I told her I was fine and that, although I did realise that Joe's reaction might *seem* a bit extreme, it was only because he was so upset.

My psychiatrist recommended a man called Theo, and a couple of days later Joe and I had a joint session with him. I don't know whether it ever crossed Joe's mind to wonder if the two therapists might be right and the intensity of his reaction wasn't entirely normal. They didn't say so in so many words, of course – Theo was just as careful and measured as Paula had been. But it was clear to me that they were both subtly implying that there might be a more constructive way of dealing with what had happened.

Joe had apparently convinced himself that I had a personality disorder, so when Theo didn't condemn my behaviour either, he made an appointment for me to see a clinical psychologist in Harley Street. When we got there, he waited downstairs while I had the assessment. But he rejected that therapist, too, when it turned out that his professional opinion didn't support Joe's diagnosis.

After that, Joe decided to take matters into his own hands and find a therapist who was nearer his own 'intellectual level', which is when he found Stephen. At least when they were discussing obscure highbrow topics Joe wasn't ranting about my deceitful immorality. Although later, when I had a session on my own with Stephen, he told me, 'You need to be careful, Alice,' and asked me if I was scared of Joe. But by that time I was *too* scared to tell the truth. So I just said what I always said in Joe's defence – that he was really upset – and ignored yet another warning.

Because Joe kept me up almost all night every night bombarding me with questions and demanding explanations, it wasn't long before I was so exhausted my work began to suffer. When I did go into the office, Joe texted me or sent me emails at regular intervals, asking more questions or telling me to meet him immediately in the small derelict courtyard at the back of the building – a place where people hardly ever went. If I didn't answer, or if I dared to say that I was busy and couldn't go, he phoned me – and kept on phoning me until I gave in.

Every morning he synchronised our watches so that I would have no excuse to be late when he told me to meet him in the courtyard at a particular time. When I got there first, which I almost always did, I would rest my head against the rough brick wall and think about the days before the discovery. About how we always took separate lifts when we arrived at work in the mornings, so as not to arouse the interest of our colleagues, and how I would step into one while Joe stood outside and mouthed 'I love you' just as the doors were closing. Then I would catch sight of my reflection in the mirrored walls, realise I was smiling, and wonder how, in just a few short weeks, I'd become happier than I had ever been in my life before. They were memories that would end abruptly when the door to the courtyard banged open and I'd feel my chest tighten as Joe walked towards me. Then we'd stand against the back wall of the office building, out of sight of the windows, while he questioned some detail or demanded an apology – for maybe the hundredth time – for something I'd done, which had to be said in exactly the right tone of voice, using exactly the right words.

'I need to know, Alice,' he'd say. 'I need to know if there were tissues on the bedside table in the hotel you stayed at when you were working with Anthony.'

'What? Tissues?' I'd be genuinely bemused. 'I … I don't know. Does it matter?'

'Of course it matters,' he would snap at me.

'But it was a year before we even met, Joe. I don't understand what difference it would make to anything.'

If it wasn't tissues on a bedside table, it was something else, equally trivial in the greater scheme of things, but apparently just as important, for whatever reason, to Joe. I often attempted to explain to him that I was *trying* to remember accurately, but that some of the things he wanted to know about hadn't been significant to me at the time. And sometimes, when I felt totally shattered and couldn't remember the detail he was questioning me about, I was tempted to lie – surely any answer was as likely to satisfy or enrage him as any other. But if I did lie,

I might not remember later what I'd said, and then, when he asked me again, as he was bound to do, I might say something different, and he'd fly into a rage and keep me awake all night until panic and exhaustion made me unable to sort out fact from fiction.

'And who is Clive?' he asked me one day. 'Why did you send him a text saying, "That's amazing. Looking forward to catching up. X"?'

'Clive?' So far beyond exhaustion and so desperate for it all to stop, I couldn't immediately put a face to anyone called Clive. And then I remembered. 'He's a friend,' I said. 'I worked with him at a gallery once. I haven't texted him for months, since long before I met you.'

'So why the kiss, Alice? You didn't mention a Clive among your past boyfriends. But if he wasn't a boyfriend, why would you have sent him such a flirty text? And why would you add a kiss?'

'It isn't a flirty text.' I hadn't ever really understood before I became the subject of Joe's questioning what it meant to experience despair. I was sobbing as I sank to my knees on the broken tiles of the courtyard floor. But if Joe ever did have the capacity to feel pity for another human being, he didn't have it then. 'Clive is just a friend, Joe. I put kisses on the end of texts to all my friends. You do it too. I've seen it. Everyone does it. What's wrong with it?'

'What's wrong with it?' Joe's voice was almost a snarl as he repeated my question. 'I'll tell you what's wrong with it, Alice. It's highly inappropriate. But I don't suppose that's something that would be obvious to an amoral whore.'

As he ranted on and on, his rage expanded into a frenzy of furious resentment. And while he berated me, I thought about the throbbing in my head and wondered if it was going to develop into the fierce headache I had almost daily now, because of all the crying and lack of sleep.

On one occasion when we met in the courtyard and he was spitting obscenities at me – calling me an evil, amoral, abhorrent whore – the fire exit door suddenly opened and someone I didn't know took a step outside. Without missing a beat, Joe switched from snarling in my face to talking in a calm, pleasant voice. I don't know if the man realised anything was amiss, or if his intention was merely to give us some privacy, but he said something to Joe I couldn't hear, then turned around and went back into the building.

Throughout those early days after the discovery, I kept thinking I'd eventually say something that would make Joe realise he was being unreasonable. It did sometimes cross my mind to wonder if *this* was the real Joe, and not the caring, loving, almost perfect man I'd known for the first five weeks of our relationship. But then I would remember that Joe had trusted me and I had broken his trust and that really *I* was the monster in the nightmare we were living in, not him.

In the meantime, it was impossible for me to do any work at all. Even during the brief periods when I was at my desk, I couldn't focus or concentrate on what I was meant to be doing. And not only did I look terrible, but it was embarrassing to be leaping up and leaving my desk every time my phone buzzed – which it did constantly – and then to return with my face red from crying. The people who worked at the desks near mine must have thought I'd completely lost the plot. But no one ever asked me any questions, or said anything at all. They just focused more intently on their computer screens and pretended they hadn't noticed that I had left my desk or returned to it.

It was all right for Joe: as head of a department he worked to his own schedule, and if he wanted to leave his desk every few minutes no one was going to ask him why. But if I didn't do the work I was supposed to be doing, or if word got round that I was acting in a very peculiar way, as it eventually must, I could lose my job. It was a Catch-22, though, because if I didn't meet Joe in the courtyard every time he told me to I would lose my job anyway – he would make sure that I did.

It began to seem as though he was spiralling out of control, transforming from 'the perfect boyfriend' into a vindictive, emotionally abusive bully. I couldn't see any way out of the nightmare I thought I'd created. And, even if I'd wanted to, I couldn't have told anyone at work what he was doing, because I knew no one would take my word against his. I couldn't escape by going home to my parents, because I knew my mother wouldn't ever forgive me for having an affair with a married man. And I still believed – still *had* to believe – that if I tried long and hard enough, I would find a way of fixing what I'd broken with my lies, and of making Joe better.

Within about a month of the discovery I was rarely going to work at all, and on the days when I did go in I did precious little that was of any use to anyone. I think Joe must have said something to my boss – who was below him in the hierarchy at work – because I wasn't ever questioned about my absences, although I knew it was a situation that couldn't last for much longer. Then, one evening, Joe said he thought I should take sick leave. 'Send an email to your boss,' he told me, 'explaining that you're going to have to take some time off work because you're suffering from depression.'

It was true that I was very upset by what was happening, but I don't think I was clinically depressed at that time. And Joe's insistence that I should give that as the reason seemed doubly cruel in view of the fact that no one at work knew that I'd ever suffered from it. But I sent the email to my boss, and he was as sympathetic and understanding as I knew he would be, telling me to take off as much time as I needed.

Joe told me a couple of days later that he had spoken to

my boss himself, to explain the situation. I only communicated with her by email during that period, so I don't know if what Joe said was true, but the thought of them discussing my 'depression' made me feel embarrassed and humiliated.

About two weeks later I sent another email to my boss – again at Joe's insistence – saying that, due to my depression, I had decided that I was going to have to hand in my notice. I *really* didn't want to give up the job, but I had struggled to do any work at all on the days when I had gone in, so there didn't seem to be any alternative.

I had been working on short-term contracts, spending just a few weeks with a particular team before moving on to work with another, and I had already become a bit isolated from the team of people I'd been working with when I met Joe. So although a couple of them did phone, I didn't pick up, because I couldn't face the thought of having to explain why I was leaving.

You can't say someone 'made' you do something. I could have said no to Joe. I could have told him that I'd worked very hard to get to where I was and that I loved my job – or had done until then. In fact, I had said no to him countless times, but he'd always worn me down, and I no longer had either the physical or mental energy required to argue a coherent case against abandoning the career that meant so much to me. And he wouldn't have listened to me if I had.

Trying to find some positive aspect of the decision Joe had made on my behalf, I told myself that at least when I was no longer working I'd have some time alone, to sleep and then maybe to think more clearly. I should have realised he wouldn't have insisted on my giving up my job if he thought it would result in his releasing even the smallest degree of the control he had over me. So I still got up every morning when he did, after an almost sleepless night of questioning and pleading. Then I drove him to the office, drove back to his house, did the shopping, cleaning and cooking, and drove to the office again to pick him up at whatever time he'd decided to come home – which could be at five o'clock in the afternoon or just an hour after I'd dropped him off. And when I wasn't doing any of those things, I was writing, then re-writing, the accounts I had to send him by email at intervals throughout the day.

While Joe was at work, every minute of my day had to be accounted for. He sent me texts and phoned at least once an hour, wanting to know what I was doing and where I was. I couldn't go anywhere without his permission – although, in reality, I was often alone in the house, with no physical constraints to hold me there, and could easily have opened the front door and walked away. But it was as though Joe had built an invisible wall around me, or brainwashed me into believing that such a wall existed. So although part of me wanted desperately to escape from the crazy, sleep-deprived, emotionally overloaded routine that had taken over our lives, another part of me wanted to stay. Because I believed I could fix Joe? Or because I thought I deserved the misery he was putting me through? I still don't know the answer to those questions.

In fact, I did *try* to leave, on more than one occasion. But he always seemed to phone just as I was plucking up the courage to open the front door, and by the time the call ended I no longer had the will or the energy required to get away. Then, one early afternoon, I finally made the decision to go. I'd put the few things I might need – money, phone, debit card – in my handbag and was actually holding the latch on the front door when it opened. 'Where are you going?' Joe asked, in a voice that made it clear that, wherever I had been going, I wasn't going there any more. 'Just to get a coffee,' I told him. And there it was, another lie told with a conviction that seemed to prove what Joe believed about me was true. Where would I have gone anyway? What I should have done, of course, was go to friends.

After the discovery, Joe had cracked the screen on my iPhone by throwing it on the floor in a rage. Then he'd given me a hammer and told me to destroy the phone, and I'd vented my frustration and distress by smashing it into a thousand pieces, sending shards of metal and glass skittering across the ground like sparks. He'd let me keep the SIM card, though – after he'd copied and then deleted the phone numbers of past boyfriends and anyone else he didn't think I should continue to have contact with. So I put that into the replacement phone he bought me, which had no internet connection and which he checked every day. Although I still had my best friend Sarah's phone number, Joe had been so irritated by her pragmatic response to the news of my affair that I didn't dare try to make contact with her. I rarely spoke to my family either, after Joe's revelation to my mother, and when I did talk to any of them on the phone I told them we were working things out and that I was 'fine', or at least soon would be.

Within just a few days of the discovery I felt as though I had no one to turn to and nowhere else to go. Already, the whole focus of my life had become Joe-and-me, and the more isolated I became, the less contact I had with anyone who might have been able to make me see that Joe's viewpoint wasn't reasonable.

My parents would have had me home if I'd asked them. But what benefit would have been gained from going from one place where I was perceived to be an awful, amoral person, to another? So I stayed with Joe, watched him dry retching and vomiting while he tore himself – and me – apart, and believed that things couldn't get any worse. Once again, however, it turned out that I was wrong.

Chapter 6

One day, Joe told me to write a list of things I could do for him and gifts I could buy that would prove how much I loved him. 'They have to be unusual and original,' he said. 'It shouldn't be difficult to think of things, unless, of course, you don't really know me at all.' But it *was* difficult, as it always is to come up with ideas for imaginative presents for anyone, even someone you know well. And it was particularly stressful trying to do it under pressure.

In the brief happy weeks of our relationship before the discovery, Joe and I often talked about countries we'd never been to and would like to visit, and others we wanted to go to again, together. One of the places that fell into the former category was Mexico, and taking Joe on holiday there was one of the few items on that first list of which he approved.

Joe's constant, remorseless questioning, which kept us awake for up to twenty hours every day, wasn't just driving me to the limits of my mental and physical endurance. It was making him ill too. There didn't seem to be any answer I could give to any question he asked me that would satisfy him. Although I didn't realise it at the time, I think he was searching for something he was never going to find, something that probably didn't really have anything to do with me specifically, with the affair I'd had with a married man, or with the fact that I wasn't 'the perfect woman' he'd told himself I was when we first started seeing each other.

Without the prospect of any other source of light at the end of the long, dark tunnel my deceit had forced us into, it did seem possible that a holiday might be a good idea. I paid for it, for our flights to Mexico City, the hotel we stayed in for the next ten nights, almost every meal we ate and every taxi we took. Using the money I'd saved for a deposit on a flat to try to make Joe happy was all part of proving I loved him and that I was prepared to do anything to make our relationship work. I paid it willingly too, because I was desperate not to lose him and because any price seemed a small one to pay for something that might make him realise how sorry I truly was. What I didn't realise, however, was that eventually, as my own savings were depleted, I would become financially, as well as emotionally, dependent on Joe, and then his control over me would be complete.

On the flight from London to Mexico City, I almost dared to believe that it was going to work. Joe talked about normal things in a normal voice, the way he used to do when we fell in love. But then, for no apparent reason, he suddenly started firing questions at me that would have been embarrassing even if they hadn't been asked loudly enough for the people around us to hear. He did lower his voice a bit when some of the other passengers began to look in our direction, although no one actually told him to pipe down when he shouted at me or asked if I was all right, not even any of the cabin crew.

It was a non-stop flight, which took about twelve hours, but seemed to last for an eternity, and although we did sleep for a few hours when we got to our hotel it wasn't long enough to make anything seem any better.

It was stupid to have hoped things might be better if we went on holiday: it was like leaving London with a broken leg and hoping to arrive in Mexico City to find that the shattered bone was whole again. There were times during the ten days we were there when we'd be in a beautiful old square or an art gallery or museum – places I'd read about and had always wanted to visit – and I'd think, 'I ought to be happy here.' But the reality was that, wherever we'd gone and whatever we'd been doing, I would have been too exhausted to take anything in, and Joe would still have been standing beside me, asking me questions about the past that made it impossible to focus on the present.

While we were there, Joe never left the hotel without me and I wasn't allowed to leave it without him, although I wouldn't have done so anyway, because all I wanted to do was sleep. I longed for Joe to fall asleep. When he was awake, so was I, and barely ten minutes ever passed when he wasn't berating or questioning me. I know that sounds crazy: it seems impossible that anyone could maintain such an intense barrage of verbal abuse for hour after hour, day after day – or that anyone would continue to put up with it. But I seemed to have lost the ability to think for myself. Perhaps that's what happens when people are subjected to brainwashing or to the sort of torture that keeps them awake for hours on end and then fills their head with illogical ideas that they no longer have the ability to process. Maybe only people who have been involved in abusive relationships themselves can really imagine what it was like.

There were several occasions while we were in Mexico City when Joe opened the window of our hotel room and threatened to jump out. And although part of me knew he wouldn't do it, I still loved him and was terrified in case he did.

One evening, Joe and I stumbled across a cobbled square with stone steps along one side of it and a crumbling but still beautiful church on the other. It was still quite early, but the square was already thronged with people, almost all of them local Mexicans, who were either dancing or engaged in lively conversation while they waited to be served at the makeshift bar that was doing a roaring trade in beer and tequila.

'Have you ever been anywhere like this before?' Joe put his arm around my shoulders and pulled me close to him, so that I could hear what he said above the sound of the music that was being played by a band of four men who were standing on the steps in the opposite corner of the square.

'No, never,' I said. 'It's incredible. Everything's so … *alive.*'

There were no street lamps in the square, or apparently on any of the streets around it. So there was no electric light to pollute the brilliance of the stars that filled the sky above our heads as we walked across the cobbles, found a small space on the stone steps and squeezed ourselves into it. Then we sat there, side by side, sipping the drinks Joe had bought for us and watching the dancers, some of whom seemed to move with the music as easily as breathing, while others laughed and stumbled and rarely hit a beat. There was one thing they all had in common, though – they were having fun. And so, miraculously, were Joe and I.

'Let's dance,' Joe said suddenly, grabbing my arm and pulling me to my feet.

'I'm a rubbish dancer,' I told him, following close behind him as he pushed through the crowds and on to the makeshift dance floor in the middle of the square.

'So am I,' he laughed. 'But it doesn't matter. I love you, Alice. Come on, let's have some fun.'

We were standing almost directly in front of the band, whose energy surpassed even that of the dancing crowd as they strummed and slapped their instruments and the man playing the double bass spun it around, as double-bass players always seem to do in films.

Joe put his arms around me as we danced and, for once, his body was relaxed and his eyes were full of fun and love, not angry and half-crazed as they normally were whenever he looked at me. I'd just realised that I was actually feeling happy, for the first time in weeks, when the singer in the band tapped Joe on the shoulder, shouted something in his ear and then pointed at me.

I could feel my body tense again, in anticipation of whatever new disaster was about to occur. Then I saw Joe smile and nod, and before I knew what was happening I was being whisked away by the Mexican singer, who twirled and swirled me across the cobblestones and didn't seem to mind any more than Joe had done that my feet were following some rhythm that apparently only I could hear.

When I looked across the square and saw Joe standing by the steps, still smiling, it was as if all the misery and despair of the last few weeks had simply evaporated and I wished that time would stand still, so that we could remain in the moment forever. I remember thinking as I watched him, 'We *can* get back to the way things used to be. Why did I ever doubt that we could? I made a horrible mistake, but Joe gave me a second chance, because he knows, as I do, that we are meant to be together.'

It really was a perfect evening, just like the ones Joe and I had shared before the discovery – until we got back to the hotel and the questioning began again.

The following day, Joe told to me to write a list of gifts I could buy for him while we were in Mexico. 'They don't have to be expensive,' he told me. 'Just things that prove you understand me.' But that was far more difficult than it might sound, and he was angry later, when I showed him the list I'd written, because he said that some of my suggestions simply proved that I neither understood him nor loved him.

While we were in Mexico, I also had to write yet more accounts of past events. At some point every day, Joe would lock me out of the hotel room and I'd sit on the sofa in the corridor, trying to separate what was true from what might be mistaken memories that had become confused with reality as my mind had become more befuddled.

The few thousand pounds the holiday cost me was money I'd saved originally as a deposit on a flat, which then became the money I was going to contribute towards the house Joe and I were still going to buy together, despite everything. However, it wasn't really a holiday at all: we just transported our nightmare from London to Mexico City for a few days, and then took it home with us again.

It wasn't only on aeroplanes that people tended to look the other way when they heard Joe shouting at me. When he did the same thing in a variety of public places, people rarely intervened. And when they did, I told them Joe was upset because I'd cheated on him, but that I was okay, and no, I didn't need any help, thanks. I was embarrassed by their concern, which is also why I always refused, at first, to humiliate myself by saying the things to strangers Joe sometimes told me to say, about how I had had an affair with a married man. He always wore me down in the end, though, by arguing and shouting until my embarrassment didn't matter any more. His was the stronger character, I suppose, and he didn't seem to have the capacity to feel guilt; whereas I had taken on the mantle of culpability and remorse without giving it a second thought.

For someone who likes to pass unnoticed as much as possible, the attention we attracted when he raged at me in public was another cause of distress for me. It didn't seem to matter to Joe at all what other people might think, or even that he might encounter someone he knew while he was in full spate, telling me I was a whore and asking me, yet again, 'Why?' It was as if his anger was so all-consuming that he became oblivious to the presence of other people. Or maybe he thought his own potential embarrassment was a small price to pay for my public humiliation.

Even in his own neighbourhood, Joe didn't seem to care that someone might hear him shouting at me. On one occasion he ranted at me for at least half an hour outside a café not far from his house, demanding answers to questions he'd asked thousands of times before. When he went inside to order more coffee, the woman at the next table leaned across to touch my arm and said, 'You've *got* to leave him. I'm so sorry to interfere, but I had a husband like that – and he ended up becoming very violent and trying to kill me. I know what it's like to feel as though you can't walk away. But, believe me, you can, and you *must*.'

I had been crying already, before the woman spoke to me, and the concern I could see in her eyes made me feel even more alone and defeated. 'I don't know what to say,' is all I managed to reply before Joe came out of the café and the woman turned away, I assume because she knew from her own experience what his reaction would be if he thought I'd been talking to someone without his permission.

I did think about what that woman said to me, and about the fact that she could see and was concerned by what was going on – and Joe hadn't been anywhere near his worst. But I was already far beyond the point of having any independent thoughts, or of being capable of acting on what was probably the best advice anyone has ever given me.

About a month after the discovery, we were in Joe's bedroom when he suddenly grabbed me by the throat and pushed me down on to the floor. I can't remember what triggered it, just that it was the end of another long, exhausting, question-filled day and he was in the middle of a tirade when, before I realised what was happening, he was straddling my body with his legs and pinning me down with so much force I couldn't move. I tried to prise his hands apart, but he was too strong for me and just kept squeezing, tighter and tighter until I couldn't breathe.

'Why are you lying to me, Alice?' he shouted, his face so close to mine I could feel his hot breath on my cheeks and his spit spattered my eyelids. Then he loosened his grip around my throat and for a moment I thought he'd come to his senses. But instead of standing up and letting me go, he started banging my head on the cold tiled floor, lifting it a few inches off the ground each time before smashing it down again with agonising force so that I could feel the blood pulsing in my temples and thought my skull was going to crack.

'Stop it, Joe!' My voice was rasping and barely audible. 'You're going to kill me. Please!'

'Why do you keep on lying to me, Alice?' He paused for a moment as if waiting for an answer, and then smashed my head on the floor again. 'You know I'll find out the truth in the end. I always find out the truth.'

The room was starting to spin, the pain in my head had become unbearable, and in that moment I truly did believe he was going to kill me. 'I love you, Joe,' I gasped, forcing the words out of my swollen, aching throat. 'You said you loved me too. Don't do this. Please.'

I knew no one was coming to help me, and the thought that I was going to die there that night, on the floor of Joe's bedroom, filled me with fear and sadness. In fact, I thought I'd given up when something seemed to burst inside me and I began to tug at Joe's arms with a strength that must have been born of desperation. Somehow – perhaps because he, too, thought I'd given up, so my attack took him by surprise – I managed to loosen his grip on my throat just enough to be able to take a deep breath and scream 'Help! Help me!' as loudly as I could.

It was only a few seconds before he'd regained his hold on me, then he bent down until his face was touching mine and hissed, 'Are you trying to make the neighbours hear you, Alice? Are you trying to get me into trouble? Do you want me to go to prison? Is that what you want? To ruin me?' And as he spat the words at me, he punctuated each one by lifting me up by the neck and then crashing my head down on the floor.

'Yes, I want someone to hear me,' I told him, when I could speak again. 'I want someone to stop you, Joe, because if they don't, you're going to kill me.'

I don't know whether any of the neighbours did hear

my cries for help that night. But no one came. So maybe Joe *would* have killed me if I hadn't taken the opportunity when it arose and tried to escape. Or maybe, despite the wild, crazed look in his eyes, he was actually in control of his actions the whole time.

When he stopped banging my head on the ground and started shouting at me that I was a whore and a liar, I glanced sideways and realised that we were little more than an arm's length away from the bedroom door. That's when the thought struck me that if I could somehow manage to push him off me I might be able to run down the stairs and open the front door before he caught up with me. 'You can do this, Alice,' I told myself. 'You have to get up off the floor and run to where there are people who will help you.'

So while Joe continued to scream at me, I relaxed my body and lay completely still for what felt like a very long time but was probably only a few seconds. Then, channelling all my anger into physical energy, I pushed him as hard as I could, catching him off guard so that he toppled backwards on to the floor. Somehow, despite the fierce pain in my head, I managed to stumble down the stairs and into the hallway, whispering aloud to myself as I ran, 'Damn it, Alice. Move! Get out. Don't faint now. You can do this. You *have* to do this.'

I was almost within reach of the front door when Joe grabbed me from behind and I fell, face down, on to the pale blue woollen rug that almost covered the tiled floor of the hallway. I just managed to turn over on to my back before he fell on top of me and started slamming my head on the ground again. At least this time the blows were slightly cushioned by the rug, although it still felt as though my skull was going to crack.

I'd known that I would have only one chance to escape, and having failed in the attempt I really did believe that I was going to die. I can remember looking up at the very expensive, and hideous, chandelier above Joe's head and feeling almost resigned to what was about to happen. Then something seemed to snap inside me and I started shouting at him, 'You're insane, Joe. You're evil. A psychopath.' But he was so lost in his own world of rage and resentment that I don't think he even heard me. And then, suddenly, he stood up and walked away, without saying a word.

When I sat up, very cautiously this time, the pain in my head was intense and I could feel the veins in my temples pulsating as if they were about to erupt. But it wasn't until I looked in the bathroom mirror and saw how swollen my face was that I realised just how close I had come to being seriously – possibly even fatally – injured. I was running my finger very gently and tentatively over the red marks and grazes on my neck when Joe came into the bathroom and stood behind me. He didn't apologise for what he'd done, either then or at any other time, but his anger seemed to have evaporated and he was completely calm, without even the slightest trace of the apparently uncontrollable temper that had gripped him for the last hour or more.

'I'm frightened, Joe,' I told him, wincing as I brushed away the tears that stung the broken skin as they rolled down my cheeks. 'My head really hurts and I don't feel well at all. What if an artery has burst in my brain and I have a stroke? I think I need to go to hospital and get my head looked at by a doctor.'

'Don't be silly, Alice,' he said, in the tone of voice an adult might use in response to an anxious child with an over-active imagination. 'Of course you don't need to see a doctor. That's just nonsense. Now come to bed.'

I thought Joe's attack on me that day had been an aberration, the cumulative result of lack of sleep, not enough to eat, and driving himself – as well as me – mad with his questions and unremitting analysis of every meaningless detail of every minute I'd ever spent with Anthony. It wasn't an aberration, though. It was the beginning of a new phase in our already supremely dysfunctional relationship that added physical violence to the armoury of weapons Joe was already using against me. But, even then, I didn't walk away. I suppose I'd been completely brainwashed by Joe and felt so guilty that I believed I deserved to be punished for what I'd done, and I was so exhausted I don't think I had enough energy to leave him.

If You Love Me

He was violent again the next day, and then quite regularly after that. Sometimes he pushed me up against a wall and held me there by my throat; sometimes he banged my head on the floor, as he'd done on that first occasion; and sometimes he bit me. In fact, some of the worst injuries he inflicted on me were bites – mostly on my arms, breasts and thighs – and the marks made by his teeth were clearly visible among the scratches and bruises that often covered my body.

Joe didn't seem to care how much he hurt me. It was as if he was completely impervious to my sobs and cries of pain, and to the fear he must have been able to see in my eyes whenever he assaulted me. Then, one night, he went too far and really scared me, banging my head against the bedroom wall again and again, until the room began to spin and I could feel my body going limp. What frightened me even more that night than the thought that I might lose consciousness, or that a blood vessel in my brain might burst, was the glazed, blank expression I could see in Joe's eyes, as if he wasn't really aware of what he was doing and couldn't hear me pleading for him to stop. Fortunately, he did stop, and when he released his grip around my throat I can remember curling up on the floor, where I must have fallen asleep.

Joe behaved the next morning as if nothing had happened. But I was shattered, and my head was thudding.

So after I'd driven him to work I went back to the house, crawled into bed and went to sleep.

It was almost two in the afternoon when I woke up again, and for a while I just lay there with the duvet pulled over my head, wishing I could sleep forever – until the realisation finally dawned on me that I *had* to leave.

I think I'd known for some time that Joe was dangerous. What I hadn't ever wondered about before that day, however, was how anyone could hurt someone they loved the way he hurt me and then simply walk away, without any apparent sense of remorse or regret. Joe often said that what I'd done had broken him. Well, now I was broken too. So what was the point of trying to fix him when I couldn't even fix myself? I was tired of being frightened, and I knew it was time to accept the fact that I wasn't going to be able to make everything perfect again, the way it had been for a few short weeks after we first met.

I had tried to put things right, to convince Joe I loved him and make him understand that the only reason I'd lied was because I was so afraid of losing him. But even if he was right and my affair with Anthony *was* unforgivable, I didn't deserve to be punished the way he was punishing me. No one deserved that, whatever they'd done. And with that realisation came an awareness of the fact that I needed help. Pushing back the duvet, I levered myself up and off the bed, then picked up the crumpled dress I'd worn the previous day and pulled it, very carefully, over the lumps and bruises on my head.

I'd just dropped my phone into my handbag when I thought I heard the sound of a key turn in the front door. Clutching the bag to my chest like a shield, I held my breath and listened. It was too late to wish I'd left earlier, instead of going back to bed. But it was all right; it was just my imagination. It couldn't have been Joe anyway: I wasn't due to pick him up from work for another couple of hours, and he would have phoned if he was coming home earlier.

I was still standing in the middle of Joe's bedroom when I heard the door open behind me and he said, in a soft, cold voice, 'Hello, Alice. I thought I'd come home and surprise you.'

It didn't even cross my mind that it was just a coincidence – bad timing on my part; good timing on Joe's. I thought he knew what I'd intended to do that day, and that he would always know, so there was no point trying to escape. In fact, for some reason based on twisted logic, I felt guilty for even having thought about leaving him.

Chapter 7

I don't think I can have realised at the time how vulnerable I was when I met Joe, in ways and for reasons I still don't entirely understand. It was partly due to the depression, I suppose, and to having my confidence so badly shaken when Jack left me. I assume that was why I'd got involved with a married man, although I know it isn't any excuse. The question I was to ask myself later, however, was this: was I so desperate to be loved that I closed my eyes to the fact that, during those first few weeks, Joe was, quite literally, too good to be true?

Although, at first, he just wanted to know about my relationship with Anthony, he then started questioning me – over and over again – about every boyfriend I'd ever had and every man I'd been on a date with, even once. I'd try to make him see how pointless his questions were by asking him, 'How could it matter to you where I went on a date with a man I didn't ever go out with again, long before I even met you?' But he'd just say something like, 'If you had told me the full truth immediately, I could have dealt with it. I'm staying with you because I love you and because I believe we're supposed to be together. I gave you everything, Alice, and in exchange you made me ill. Well, now you've got to make me better.'

On the days that Joe didn't go in to work, he would question me for hours on end. And when he *was* at work, I spent an increasing amount of time writing accounts of every detail of my relationship with Anthony and of every other man I'd ever dated. I didn't just write a paragraph or two; I filled page after page with dates, times, what I was wearing, where we went, what we ate, descriptions of restaurants and hotel rooms, details of every single sexual act, whether or not I'd had an orgasm, what happened afterwards … It was crazy – crazy that Joe told me to do it and perhaps even crazier that I did.

There were many reasons why I hated writing those accounts, including the fact that I'd always been a very private person and the last thing I'd have wanted to do in any circumstances was reveal details of something I was ashamed of. Sometimes, I tried to make Joe understand that I couldn't remember some of the things he asked me about. 'When you keep insisting that I describe some detail I've forgotten,' I told him, 'you're forcing me to lie and make something up.' But he would always say the same thing: 'I don't accept that, Alice. You *will* remember.

You're just not trying hard enough. How could anyone forget even the smallest detail of something so abhorrent?'

I lost count of the number of times Joe threw me out of the house quite late in the evening and I'd have to sit in the small car park that served some of the houses on our side of the street until I remembered something I hadn't mentioned in a particular account before – 'a new truth', he used to call it, although, eventually, the only way I could satisfy his expectations was by making up 'a new lie'. The problem was, if he ever caught me out in a lie, or if I misremembered some minor detail that I later corrected in one of the many updates I had to write of almost every account, I had to do a forfeit.

Joe was always coming up with new ideas about things I could do to prove I loved him. And however inexplicable or bizarre they might seem, I did them all, either because I really did believe that, *this* time, it would finally be the proof he needed, or because I was afraid of him.

One of the most humiliating things he made me do – on many, many occasions – was run through the streets in the middle of the night, wearing only my underwear or, sometimes, nothing at all. One night I was crouching behind the low stone wall that bordered the car park, naked and with my heart thudding as I checked to make sure the street was empty before I set off, when Joe crept up silently behind me and pushed me, so that I fell on to the gravel, cutting my knees and the palms of my hands quite badly. He always gave me his phone after that – there was no camera on the one he'd bought to replace my iPhone – and I had to prove that I'd run to the end of the road by taking a photograph of the pub or of a particular tree that had flowers growing around its base.

There would be a time limit too, which heightened still further the huge anxiety I always felt, because it meant that if I did hear footsteps while I was checking the street, I never knew whether the greater evil would be to risk being seen or not getting back to the house by the appointed time. It's strange when I think about that now, that I was more afraid of Joe than I was of running naked through the streets of London in the early hours of the morning.

Fortunately, the man who stepped out of the shadows in front of me one night and then staggered after me was so drunk that I managed to outrun him. I was very frightened, though, and by the time I reached Joe's house the soles of my bare feet were bruised and bleeding.

I didn't blame the drunk man for pursuing me that night, or for scaring me so badly. Even someone completely sober would probably have reacted in some way to the sight of a naked woman running through the streets of London in the early hours of the morning. The only person I blamed for anything that happened to me at that time was myself, because of what I'd done to Joe that had turned him from the perfect boyfriend into a relentless interrogator and tyrannical bully.

On another night I thought I heard someone walking towards me and had darted into a garden, where I was standing, listening, with my back pressed against the wall, when I saw a flicker of movement out of the corner of my eye. It was well past midnight and every house in the street was in darkness. But when I turned my head towards the house, I realised I was being watched.

There were no lights on in the house, but the face of the woman looking out of the uncurtained window was sufficiently illuminated by the yellow glow of a street lamp for me to be able to see the contours of her gaunt cheeks and the dark circles under her eyes. I could hear the blood pounding in my ears and for a moment I thought I was going to faint. Then I moved my head and the woman moved hers, which is when it dawned on me that there *was* no one watching me, and that the face I could see was the reflection of my own. For a split second I felt a sense of relief, until I glanced down at the watch Joe had given me, which he insisted I must wear at all times and which hung, heavy and loose, around my wrist, and realised I had just four minutes to get to the pub two streets away, take a photograph and run back to his house.

I could feel panic rising up from the pit of my stomach to form a solid lump in my throat. Then, suddenly, I felt angry. I wanted to shout into the dark silence of the night, 'I give in. You win, Joe. I can't do this any more.' But, even as the thought came into my head, I knew I *would* do what Joe had told me to do. Because I always did, and because I had just two options: I could do it now or I could do it later, after hours of relentless questioning, by which time both my mind and my body would be bruised and exhausted.

'Maybe this time,' I told myself as I turned my back on my reflection in the window, 'when I get home and show Joe yet another photograph that proves I've completed the task he set me, he'll believe I really love him and he'll forgive me.'

In comparison to the physical assaults, all the lists, letters and detailed accounts of past events Joe made me write should have been insignificant. In fact, they wore me down almost as much as the violence did. I had to write a letter to him every day, telling him why he was so special and what new sacrifice I was going to make to prove how much I loved him. When he read the letters, he criticised almost everything I'd written in them. He would accuse me of repeating myself and say things like, 'Am I supposed to believe that you love me more than you loved the married man when all you can think of to write fills just two sides of A4 paper?'

To be constantly trying – and always failing – to please Joe was exhausting and demoralising, and I'd begun to wonder if it was ever going to be possible to prove how sorry I was for what I'd done and how much I loved him.

And then there were the rules. When Joe first mentioned them as a specific entity, he talked about them as though they were the result of a joint decision, something we both thought would be useful. 'We need a set of rules about how we will both act,' he said. 'Don't you agree, Alice? What do you think the first one should be?' But there were no joint decisions by that stage, and although the Alice who'd existed before the discovery might have laughed at the suggestion that one partner in a loving relationship should have to abide by rules and regulations set by the other partner, I knew he wasn't joking.

There's no disputing the fact that I played a role in my own misery. I should have refused from the outset to do any of the things Joe demanded of me. I should have realised that his behaviour wasn't normal. But he seemed to have an uncanny ability to identify my weaknesses and vulnerabilities and then to use them, ruthlessly, to control me. There's no doubt about the fact that he was very clever, and that he manipulated me, deliberately and systematically, into giving up everything I had, so that I ended up with nothing but him. And once I'd invested everything in him, it became even more difficult for me to leave. Or, at least, that was how it seemed to me at the time.

Joe's question about what the first rule should be had been purely rhetorical, and without waiting for me to answer he suggested, 'How about that you don't go out with any males by yourself?'

'But I don't go out with anyone,' I said.

'So what are you saying?' His expression was quizzical but his voice was cold. 'Do you *want* to go out without me?'

'No, of course not. You know I don't,' I said hastily, never for a moment even considering giving in to the temptation to scream at him, 'What I want is to get away from all the madness and have a normal relationship, like other couples have who phone their families and friends and arrange to meet up – together or on their own – whenever they want to.'

Two hours later, the list was written. It was entitled 'Our Rules', although, in reality, almost every one of them referred to me.

Our Rules
- We will have no secrets.
- We will spend as much time together as possible.
- I will drive you to and pick you up from work every day.
- Every evening, when we haven't been together during the day, we will tell each other *everything* that has happened.

- I will tell you when I want to go out for coffee or lunch with anyone, and I won't go if you don't agree.
- We will not go out for coffee or lunch with anyone of the opposite sex.
- I will either phone you or send you emails at regular intervals throughout the day.
- You will have access to all my emails, both work and private.
- If you have a question about anything that's written in any of my emails, you will phone me or text me and I will meet you somewhere immediately to explain it to you.
- I will only use my phone to send texts and make phone calls.
- I will not use an iPhone or any other kind of phone that has a camera or Internet access.
- I will only access the Internet and send and receive emails on the laptop at home.
- We will never delete any texts or emails, however insignificant we think they are.
- I will not have a Facebook account, or access any other social media sites.
- Our phone bills will always be itemised.
- We will share our passwords.
- We will share diaries and contacts.
- We will tell each other in advance about any work dos that we have been asked to go to.

If You Love Me

- I will have no contact with any male friends.
- I will only contact female friends that you approve of.
- We will tell each other – truthfully – every day how we feel, good or bad.
- If we have to travel alone by public transport at any time, we will tell each other in advance where we are going and how we are going to get there. While we are travelling, we will keep in regular touch by text or phone call.
- If anyone asks us out, we will say, 'No, thank you. I already have a boyfriend/girlfriend.'
- Wherever we have been and whatever we have been doing during the day, we will not spend the night apart.
- If I ever bump into Anthony, I will ignore him and walk – or run – away. If he insists on trying to speak to me, I will phone you immediately.
- I will write to Anthony's daughter to tell her the truth about my relationship with her father.
- I will cook for you every evening.
- I will not wear padded bras.
- We will never lie to each other for any reason and in any situation, even if telling the truth will hurt the other person's feelings.
- I will try very hard to be the best girlfriend possible.
- I will do something romantic for you every day.

- I will tell you several times every day how much I love you.
- I will curb my own desires to make sex better for you.
- I will have counselling every day for the next two months, then at least three times a week for six months after that.
- In the counselling sessions, I will address issues related to my depression, self-esteem, relationships and lying.
- By a date to be decided, I will have sorted out a new career for myself.
- I will do whatever is necessary to help us find and buy a new house and will be responsible for organising our move.
- I will do everything I can to try to make you happy again.

When I'd written the list of rules, Joe read through them, and as he handed them back to me he said, 'I think this is a good idea, don't you, Alice? It's a positive step forward. But remember, if you ever lie to me again, just one single lie, I will leave you. I will leave you if you break *any* of these rules. I *will* have dark moods sometimes, which you will have to help me to get through with patience and zeal. And think about the romance too. That's going to be the bigger task, other than loyalty and not lying. Because unless you're able to make me feel very, very special every day, this isn't going to work. But if you do fulfil these requirements, Alice, I swear that, in return, I will do my best to love you.'

Calling his violent, abusive rages 'dark moods' was like calling a devastating hurricane a 'gentle breeze'. But I was so desperate to believe it was possible for me to do *some*thing that would fix the mess I thought I'd single-handedly created that I promised to stick to the rules and do everything I could think of to try to make him happy again.

It was just a few weeks after the discovery when Joe told me one day that he thought it would be a good idea if I checked myself in to a private rehab facility where they also treat a variety of clinical disorders. It was very expensive – about £700 a night – and because of my pre-existing depression my private health insurance wouldn't cover it. 'You can use your savings,' Joe said, referring to the money I'd saved up as a deposit for a flat. 'It will only be for a month or so and you did say you'd do anything to put things right.'

He didn't want me to go to the nearest place, which was where the psychiatrist I saw privately every few months was based, because he said it had links to the married man. So I went to one more than 100 miles away from London, not all that far from where my parents live.

Mum didn't know anything about the physical violence, which had only recently started, and when Joe phoned her and explained what he was suggesting and the reasons behind it – while I listened to their conversation on speaker phone – she agreed that it was a good idea. Even by that time, I thought *he* needed professional help more than I did. But I was desperate to get some respite from the torture of his constant questioning and abuse, and if the only way I was going to be able to escape was by paying nearly £5,000 a week, then I was willing to give it a try.

Joe stood on the platform at the station in London until my train began to move. Then Mum met me at the other end and, during the miserable drive to the clinic, told me again how upset she was by what I'd done and by the fact that my life was in such a shambles. I couldn't argue with her appraisal of my situation, which seemed to be pretty much that I'd got myself involved in a sordid affair, had potentially ruined a family, and had then lied to a lovely man. Or with her apparent view that this might be my last chance to sort my life out. But by the time we arrived at the clinic I felt as though I was the worst person in the world.

Although it was true that I had underlying depression and that I was feeling more miserable than usual, both things seemed understandable in the circumstances, and I'd been certain that the whole idea of going to the clinic – not to mention spending all that money – was crazy. But that brief car journey with my mother did make me start to doubt my own sanity.

When we arrived at the clinic, I was checked in and then had a brief meeting with a doctor. 'She's had an affair with a married man,' Mum told him, almost as soon as we'd sat down. And although his expression remained neutral, he turned slightly away from her when he asked me, 'Why do you think you need to be here, Alice?'

'I don't know that I do need to be here,' I answered. 'Although I *do* have depression.'

'Well, let's see, shall we?' the doctor said. 'We'll do an assessment tomorrow and then take things from there.'

Mum said some other things I can't remember now. But I know she was anxious, not least because I don't think she'd even considered the possibility that they might decide I didn't need to be there, which to her meant I might not get the help she was so certain I needed. And the doctor's tone was cool when he suggested that it might be time for her to go, so that I could settle in.

A very nice nurse took me up to my room, which was small, clean and comfortable, with an en-suite bathroom, deliberately bland artwork on the walls, a flat-screen TV, a private phone and a vase of fresh flowers on the bedside table. Everything about it was pleasant but characterless – like most hotel rooms – and in stark contrast to the spectacular view from its window of the fields and woodland surrounding immaculately manicured lawns.

What the room didn't have, however, was a mobile phone signal. So by the time Joe had called reception and been put through on the landline, he was in a foul temper. Having a phone in my room meant I could make calls that Joe would have no way of tracing. So after he'd vented his frustration for a while and then rung off, I phoned my friend Sarah and told her where I was. 'You don't need to be there, Alice,' she said emphatically. 'You had an affair. That's all. Although it wasn't a great idea, you aren't the first person to have done it, and you certainly won't be the last. But maybe staying there for a couple of days will enable you to get some rest and give you the chance to talk to some people who'll be able to convince you that, whatever Joe might say or think, you are completely sane.'

I had to cut the call to Sarah short, because I was afraid Joe might be trying to get through on the landline again – which, having realised that he could dial my room direct, he did constantly for the next three or four hours. Apparently, it's standard practice to check on new patients at regular intervals during the first 24 hours after admission. And when one of the night-shift nurses came in and found me weeping and on the phone yet again, she took the handset from me and told Joe, 'Alice is exhausted and you're making her really upset. You need to stop calling now so that she can get some sleep.' She didn't know what was going on and I don't know what Joe said to her, but I was so grateful to have someone to speak up for me that I hugged her when he hung up – although he phoned again very shortly afterwards.

When I woke up the next morning, I had a shower and then went to the dining room and tried to eat some breakfast. I'd only just returned to my room when there was a knock on the door and a man who introduced himself as Dr Clifford asked if he and his colleague could come in and do their initial assessment.

I motioned them towards the two chairs, then sat on the bed with my legs crossed under me, feeling like a small, disorientated child. I couldn't believe I was in a hospital – or a clinic, as the staff preferred to call it. What had happened to my life? Just a few weeks ago, I'd been happy. I'd had a great job, a good social life, and had been on the verge of buying my own flat. It was true that my 'love life' hadn't been going so well and that I didn't have a boyfriend, despite telling myself that Anthony and I were … 'something'. Other than that, though, I'd had pretty much everything else I could have wanted. Then I'd found Joe and suddenly *everything* had been perfect. Could I really have lost it all by doing something so stupid as lying about my affair with a married man to the only man who had ever really mattered to me?

'So tell me, Alice …' I could feel my face flush with embarrassment when I realised Dr Clifford was speaking to me – being lost in a world of my own wasn't the best way to convince him that I was sane. 'Why are you here? What brought you to our clinic? It says on your notes that you've suffered from depression for the last fifteen years.'

He tapped his pen on the pad of paper that was resting on his knees and smiled at me. It was a friendly smile, and his colleague seemed nice too. So why did I feel so nervous now?

I stretched out my arm to pick up the glass from the table beside the bed and took a gulp of water. What should I tell them? The truth about Joe? About the abuse and violence that never stopped except when he was asleep? Or should I lie to protect him? They were clearly sensible, intelligent people. So the obvious answer was to tell them the truth. But what if Joe was right and *I* was the one who was to blame for everything? What if I *had* made him ill and all the things I was doing for him now *did* eventually make him better? If that happened, I'd get the old Joe back and everything would be all right again. More than all right, in fact: perfect.

'I don't need to be here.' The words burst out of me in short, staccato bursts. 'I don't *want* to be here. Yes, I do have depression, but ...' The two doctors nodded their heads in unison and suddenly I decided there would be no more lies; no more believing I was crazy and Joe wasn't; and no more spending all the money I'd worked so hard to save on help I didn't need.

Taking a deep breath, I told them, 'It's my boyfriend, Joe. Well, Joe and my mother. They're the ones who think I need to be here.' Then I explained the whole story, about how I met Joe, how he'd found out about Anthony, how he'd reacted when he discovered I'd had an affair with a married man, and how his reaction, coupled with my mother's disgust and condemnation, had made me feel that what I'd done was so unforgivable I had to find some way to make amends.

It was as if, once I started talking, I couldn't stop. The one thing I couldn't bring myself to tell the two doctors, however, was about the physical abuse. Everything else was explicable – extreme maybe, but understandable on some level; whereas telling them about Joe's violence would have felt like the ultimate betrayal.

'I know what I did was wrong,' I said. 'And I understand that Joe has been very badly hurt by it. But I think that the deep unhappiness I feel now is a natural reaction to everything that's happened, and not – as Joe and my mother believe – a sign that I'm clinically depressed.'

'You're not a terrible person, Alice,' Dr Clifford said when I eventually paused to draw breath. 'These things happen – for all sorts of reasons. So don't keep punishing yourself for it. You know it was a mistake. And I think you also know that Joe and your mother are overreacting to quite a considerable degree. I don't think you need to be here, and I'm more than happy for you to leave. But you *do* need to sort out your relationship with Joe. It isn't healthy. In fact, it's abusive and wrong. You must be able to work and see your friends.'

The relief I felt as I listened to what the doctor was saying was like a physical sensation – coming up for air, for example, after you've been swimming underwater for almost too long. As I leaned back against the headboard of the bed, I felt calm for the first time in weeks: if two qualified, experienced doctors thought I was sane and not one of the most horrible, amoral people who had ever walked the earth, maybe Joe and my mother were wrong.

I turned my head and looked out of the window at the fields beyond the lawns and flowerbeds. 'That's where I want to be,' I thought. 'Walking in the countryside with the sun on my back. Not shut up inside a clinic. And certainly not in Joe's house, cataloguing the details of all my past crimes and constantly on edge, waiting for the moment when something would trigger a thought or a memory and he would lash out at me, banging my head against the wall or the floor until I thought I was going to die. I was tired of blaming myself for whatever was wrong with Joe, and for being blamed by him. I had tried my best to fix what I thought I'd broken, and now I wanted to live a normal life. I shouldn't ever have listened to Joe or my mother. I should have followed my own instincts, which told me that I didn't need to be in a clinic and which had now been confirmed by two very expensive medical opinions!

What happened to my thought processes in the relatively brief period between having that conversation with Dr Clifford and his colleague and signing out of the clinic,

I don't know. I didn't feel I could go home to my parents, not least because I knew my mother wouldn't agree with the doctors' assessment and I didn't want to see her look at me as though I was an impostor who'd been pretending to be someone she knew and loved. But I could have phoned my friend Sarah and gone to her flat, where I'd have been safe.

I didn't do that, though. In fact, I didn't do any of the things you'd expect a sane, rational person to do. Instead, I got a taxi to the local railway station and then phoned Joe to tell him I was on my way home. He wasn't angry with me, as I thought he would be, and he didn't say, 'Don't come back.' Perhaps he'd realised that while I was at the clinic he wouldn't have total control over me, the way he had at home, and that other people would be influencing my thoughts and decisions, so it was better to have me back.

He didn't say he was pleased to see me, either, when the taxi I took from the station in London dropped me off outside his house. I think the only reference he made to my having been away at all was to say, 'You're going to have to work really hard at being back,' which made me feel as though I ought to be grateful to him for the huge sacrifice he was making by letting me return. But it was okay, because having proved – to myself, at least – that I wasn't crazy, I was quite prepared to do whatever it took to help Joe to become sane again too.

Sometimes, when I was struggling to believe that things could ever be the way they were, I would remember the night when Joe and I ran up the hill in the park together, then stood in the darkness at the top, his arms wrapped tightly around me as he kissed me and told me he loved me. I thought about it that day, when I was sitting in the taxi on my way back to Joe's house, and it made me feel strong enough to believe that I could help him finally come to terms with what had happened, and fix what I had broken. Perhaps, if I hadn't been as fragile as I really was, I would have realised that the situation was far more serious than I imagined.

Chapter 8

I'd accepted by that time that everything Joe and I did, even everyday things like grocery shopping, was going to involve me defending myself against his verbal and, now, physical attacks. What was even more surreal, however, was doing things with him like buying a Christmas tree – things that had been special to me ever since I was a little girl – while he kept up a constant barrage of questions about the past. I had always gone home for Christmas; even when I was with Jack I hadn't spent a single Christmas away from my family. But not long after my very brief admission to the private clinic, Joe and I spent our first Christmas together alone, at his house.

For two normally quite decisive people, it took us a ridiculous amount of time to choose a tree. We spent ages walking along rows of different types of spruce, fir and pine trees, examining the shape and height of each one until we found one that was perfect in every respect, although perhaps a bit on the tall side for a tree that wasn't going to stand in the middle of Trafalgar Square! While we were struggling back to the car with it, we passed a woman with a little boy, who pointed at it and said, 'I want a Christmas tree just like that,' which made me smile – something I very rarely did by that time.

In fact, the tree we'd chosen was too big to fit in Joe's car. So we had to leave the boot open and tie ropes around it to stop it falling out on the way home. We were picking pine needles out of the car for days afterwards, and out of the carpet in the house too. But it fitted perfectly in the living room, when we finally managed to manoeuvre it into the space we'd cleared for it. And it looked beautiful when we finished decorating it, with glass balls and clear white lights.

Christmas was a stressful time, though – even more so than every other waking minute of every other day – because I knew Joe was expecting the presents I bought for him to be innovative and original, the sort of presents that would prove I wasn't 'a shallow person', he told me. Which meant that even spending a lot of money on them was no guarantee that I wouldn't get it wrong.

I can't remember now what I bought for Joe. I do know, though, that as I wrapped up his presents in the paper I'd chosen so carefully, I felt excited because I was convinced he'd be pleased with them. I was wrong, of course. 'You don't know me at all,' was all he said after he'd opened the first one. And then, later, 'If you loved me as much as you say you do, you'd have put more thought and effort into choosing the presents you bought.'

The present Joe bought for me was a SousVide, an expensive piece of kitchen equipment for cooking vacuum-sealed food in a water bath. It wasn't something I'd ever expressed any interest in having. But I suppose if I *had* been the perfect woman Joe was trying to mould me into, I would have been as delighted with it as I told him I was.

I don't know why I allowed myself to have any expectations about Christmas being different from any other day. I didn't spend it with my family – who thought I'd stayed in London with Joe because that was where I wanted to be – and I didn't see any of my friends either. In fact, I hadn't even spoken to any of them for weeks. No antidepressant has ever been developed that would have made me feel better about what my life had become, and on Boxing Day, when the violence and questioning became too much, I took a handful of tablets.

I can still remember the feeling of despair that overwhelmed me as I sat on the edge of the bed with tears streaming down my cheeks and swallowed first one tablet, then another, and then three more, before washing them all down with a generous quantity of red wine. The fact that I told Joe what I'd done seems to confirm the possibility that I didn't really intend to kill myself. So maybe it was just a cry for help. But although he phoned my mother, he wasn't worried at all; just angry. Mum was distraught, though, not least because she thought it was a recurrence of the depression I'd had as a student. 'You must call the crisis team,' she told Joe, her voice like an echo inside my head as I listened on speaker phone. 'She needs help.'

'Of course I bloody well need help,' I wanted to shout at her. 'But *I* don't need the crisis team. *He* does. Can't anyone see that?' Mum didn't know about the violence at that point, or even about the constant mental abuse Joe was subjecting me to. And although I wanted to tell her what was happening, that everything wasn't quite as simple as it seemed, and that Joe wasn't the wounded martyr he appeared to be, I didn't say anything. Maybe I was angry with her because I thought she should be on my side automatically, without my needing to explain. Looking back on it now, though, I suppose she *was* on my side, in her own way. She was certainly very distressed when she eventually found out the truth about how Joe had been treating me. But when he made that phone call to her, she still believed I was the only guilty party and Joe the only victim in our relationship.

Calling the crisis team would have been the last thing Joe wanted to do, in case it resulted in the truth coming out. So he persuaded my mother that it wasn't necessary and that he had everything under control. And because he was very good at manipulating people into believing whatever suited his purposes, I think she felt relieved to know that I was being looked after by someone so capable and caring.

I did open my mouth to say something when I heard the panic in Mum's voice that day. But I suddenly felt very hot and sweaty, and the room seemed to be filling up with a dense white fog that muffled Joe's voice, making it sound distant and indistinct. So instead of trying to speak to my mum, I told myself, 'It's all right. Just keep very still and be very quiet. You're not going to die. It's the booze and tablets making you feel this way. But don't worry. Everything's going to be okay.' And, for once, I was right – about not dying, at least, although not about everything being okay.

After Christmas, Joe and I went on holiday to Greece, which was another country we'd talked about visiting together during the early days of our relationship. I hadn't ever been to Greece before, but Joe had, with his wife – a fact which, oddly perhaps, hadn't put me off his idea of us getting married there. Even more bizarrely, getting married was still something Joe and I planned to do, a few months after the discovery and several weeks after the first of his violent physical attacks. Not on this occasion, though; this time it was just a holiday, paid for, once again, out of my savings – out of the money I hadn't had to spend on a month's stay at a private clinic, I suppose.

Within hours of arriving at Athens International Airport, Greece had become another place – like Mexico – that I'd always wanted to visit but never wanted to see again. Not because of the place itself, which was beautiful; but because I was even more miserable there with Joe than I was at his house in London. We were staying in a hotel just a stone's throw from the beach in a village a few kilometres from Athens itself. On any normal holiday you couldn't have wished for a more tranquil, relaxing and picturesque setting. For me, though, the only difference from being in London was that, as I didn't speak the language, I felt even more isolated and unable to ask for help, should the need arise.

Joe's interminable questioning continued while we were in the hotel, walking by the sea, and visiting the sights in Athens I'd always wanted to see and was now barely aware of. In the evenings, we sat in bars and restaurants, where the crouched intensity of our verbal exchanges was punctuated at intervals by Joe's aggressive shouting, much to the embarrassment of the people at the tables around us.

One evening, I think it was the third or fourth after we'd arrived, we were sitting in a bar when Joe started fumbling with a match, trying to light a cigarette. The fact that he liked smoking but rarely did it was another aspect of the tight control he exerted over almost all his actions. For some reason, though, he'd bought a pack of cigarettes earlier that evening, and had already smoked four of them.

When someone opened the door to the street, a gentle gust of air snuffed out the first match Joe struck. And as I watched him light another, I thought how handsome he was and how I'd give anything to be able to turn back the clock and to be sitting there with him having never met Anthony, and therefore having never told him a lie. 'If it wasn't for my affair with Anthony,' I thought, 'Joe and I would be sitting here laughing and talking to each other the way we did on our first holiday together in Barcelona, when everything was perfect.' Instead of Joe shouting at me and demanding meaningless answers to pointless questions, we'd be discussing how many children we were going to have and the dog we were going to get – not a handbag-sized pedigree dog, we'd both agreed, but a decent-sized, slightly scruffy and mischievous mutt that would bound up the hill in the park when we took it for a walk. We'd been so certain we were right for each other, I thought. Surely it wasn't too late to go back to the way we were then.

When Joe finally managed to light his cigarette, I held my breath as I watched the smoke curl across the table towards me, knowing that he'd be irritated if I coughed or turned away. Then, suddenly, I realised he was speaking to me.

'I … I'm sorry, Joe,' I said. 'I was watching the smoke. What did you say?'

'I said, I want you to get drunk.'

'No. No, I won't do it,' I told him, emphatically. 'You know more than a couple of glasses of wine have a bad effect on me. I did it last night and the night before that because you asked me to. But I'm not doing it again.' It was true that I'd got drunk on the last two nights, because Joe had coerced and bullied me until I gave in. Then he'd questioned me until the early hours of the morning about things that shouldn't have mattered to him and certainly hadn't ever mattered to me. It seemed to have become an addiction for Joe, though, asking me the same questions over and over again, demanding that I answer them every time in the same way, using the same words, articulated in the same tone of voice. But even when I did exactly what he asked me to do, he was never satisfied – any more than any type of addict is ever satisfied by just one more fix, I suppose.

'If you love me, you'll get drunk tonight. You got drunk for him,' Joe said. 'You were drunk that first night, the night you got involved with him. Isn't that how the whole sordid, amoral affair began? So don't tell me you won't get drunk for me now.' His voice grew louder and more aggressive with every word he spoke, and he was swearing too, emphasising each profanity with furious hostility.

Although I cried and pleaded with him, Joe remained coldly impassive, as unmoved as he always was by my tears and distress. We were in a foreign country, he had all the money and my passport, and I had nowhere to go, except back to our room at the hotel, where no one would see him become violent and where there would be no one to intervene when he started strangling and hitting me. I didn't think he would attack me in public, however out of control he might seem to be. So at least I wasn't in any physical danger while we were in the bar, where some of the people at the tables around us were already glancing quizzically in our direction whenever he raised his voice. Would they help me if I asked them to, I wondered? I thought they probably would. But what was the point of asking for help when I knew I would end up siding with Joe so that he didn't get into trouble for reacting to the pain I believed I alone had caused him?

Suddenly, I longed for normality: to be able to respond to anyone who spoke to me, wherever and whoever they were; to have a drink with colleagues after work; to talk to friends about all the mundane, inconsequential things that are part of conversation in normal daily life; and to think about my life before Joe without feeling ashamed because I believed I was a horrible person. Just thinking about all those things and wondering if I would ever be able to do them again seemed to absorb the last remnants of my energy.

'Fine,' I said to Joe, wiping away the tears with the back of my hand. 'I'll have one more drink.' Because you'll win this argument like you win them all, I could have said, and because maybe the sooner I drink it, the sooner this night will be over.

'You'll drink as many as I tell you to.' Joe's voice was harsh and cold, although it lightened as he raised his hand to attract the attention of the waitress and added, 'Now, let's drink.'

The more Joe drank, the more persistent and bizarre his questioning became, and the more violent his behaviour. But I didn't ask him to stop drinking, because I knew that doing so would only make things worse.

Many, many questions later, we had left the bar and were walking back to the hotel along cobbled streets, which were surprisingly full of people for four o'clock in the morning, when Joe asked, 'Why did you take your jeans off that first night you spent with him?'

'Because I'm a whore,' I wanted to shout at him. 'Because I'm an amoral, unprincipled, family-crushing prostitute. Is that what you want me to tell you?' But that, too, would have just made everything worse, and I knew already that it was going to be a very long night.

When Joe suddenly pushed me, I sat down heavily on a stone step beside a doorway and he knelt on the pavement in front of me, pressing my back against the sharp, uneven bricks of the wall as he screamed into my face. I hadn't ever heard anyone else scream the way Joe did. It wasn't like normal shouting or yelling; it was more high-pitched, like a verbalised, almost hysterical, cry of pain. He was calling me terrible names, accusing me of terrible things, and breathing hot, cigarette-laden breath into my face until I thought I was going to be sick. Although I tried to push him away, the alcohol he'd drunk and the fury that was never far below the surface of his demeanour gave him an irresistible strength. So I cowered against the wall, clutching my arms around my knees, longing, but not daring, to plead for help from the people walking past.

Some people did stop and watch us with expressions of concern. But none of them intervened in what must have looked to them like a heated argument between two equally drunk foreigners. Then Joe started biting me, first on my arm, then on my chest and breasts, sinking his teeth into the tender flesh and ignoring my cries of pain and pleas for him to stop. A small crowd of people had gathered on the pavement in front of us by that time, but still no one intervened or tried to help me, although perhaps one of them was responsible for alerting the two police officers who suddenly appeared beside us and asked me, in English, if I was all right.

I could feel Joe's eyes on me, daring me to answer. But he didn't have to worry. What I wanted to say to the police officer was, 'Please, help me. Can't you see this man is crazy?' But I was so shocked and distressed, and so befuddled by alcohol, that I just sat there at the side of the road, sobbing hysterically and pressing the palms of my hands on to the red marks left by Joe's teeth and the painful lacerations on my breasts.

'It's okay,' Joe said imperiously, acknowledging the police officers at last. 'She's okay.' Then he turned to me and said, 'Come on, Alice. Let's get back to the hotel.'

He looked angry, as though he thought I was entirely to blame for the police officers' presence, because I hadn't sat there silently at the side of the road while he bit and assaulted me. Seeing the look in his eyes was what made me realise that, whatever happened, I mustn't go back to the hotel with him that night, where there would be no other people and where I knew I would not be safe.

Somehow, I managed to stand up, and as I did so one of the police officers took an almost imperceptible step forward, placing himself between me and Joe as he asked me, 'Can I speak with you – alone?' I nodded, ignoring the warning look Joe gave me before he allowed himself to be led across the street by the other officer.

'What happened to your arm?' The policeman asked me, as soon as Joe was out of earshot. 'Are you hurt?'

Maybe I'm particularly susceptible to guilt. Maybe Joe realised that and used it to his advantage, to enable him to manipulate and control me the way he did. I don't know why that might be the case, but I can't think of any other reason for feeling as though I was to blame for almost everything bad that ever happened. I sometimes wonder if Joe could have selected a news report at random about some catastrophic event that had occurred somewhere in the world and then persuaded me to believe that I was responsible for it. I certainly felt responsible for anything bad that happened to him, which was why I was so anxious that night about the possible repercussions for him if I told the truth. Would he be arrested, and maybe end up in a prison in Greece? If that did happen, it might ruin his career, which in turn would compound the harm I believed I'd already done to him. So, instead of saying, 'Yes, I *am* hurt. My body is covered with cuts and bruises. I need to get away from this man. I need your help. Don't leave me alone with him. *Please*,' I covered the marks on my chest with my hands and said, 'No, I'm not hurt. It's nothing.'

'What is your name?' the man asked me. 'Where are you from?'

'My name is Alice Keale,' I said. 'I'm from London.'

He wrote something in his notebook and when he looked at me again there was an expression of genuine concern in his eyes as he said, 'You looked frightened. You sounded frightened, too. What was going on?'

But it was too late. The moment had passed when I might have helped myself. My instinct for self-preservation, along with my determination not to go back to the hotel with Joe that night, had once again been swamped by the feeling of guilt that always placed his well-being above my own and made me believe that, if I loved him enough, the nightmare we were living would come to an end. So I told the officer that I was fine. 'We had an argument,' I said. 'It's nothing really. I'm so sorry to have wasted your time. It was my fault.'

When the police officers let us go and we were walking back to the hotel, Joe asked me, 'What name did you give them?'

'*My* name,' I said, bemused by the question. 'Why? What name did *you* give them?'

'A fake one, you fool! I don't believe it, Alice.' Joe was instantly furious again. 'Are you trying to get me into trouble? Is that what you want to do? Why would you do that to me when it's all your fault? When everything is your fault?'

Why hadn't I thought to give a fake name too, I wondered. It was a mistake I paid the price for that night when we were alone in our room at the hotel and Joe punctuated each question and accusation he spat at me by banging my head on the floor.

We went on other holidays and trips abroad after Greece, while my savings lasted – to Paris for just one night to see a ballet at the Palais Garnier, to Capri for a few days, and to Rome for a week. I don't know how long it was, and how many holidays we'd been on, before I allowed myself to wonder if there was ever going to be anything I could do to convince Joe that I loved him as much as he'd believed I did during the first few weeks of our relationship, before the discovery. I hadn't completely lost faith in the possibility by the time we went to Rome, although I came close to it on the second evening we were there. We were sitting outside a café near the Piazza Navona when Joe suddenly said that he wanted me to buy him ten unique and original gifts.

'You don't mean *now*?' I asked him. But of course he did.

'You've got more than an hour before the shops shut,' he said. 'That's plenty of time.'

'I'm not doing it.' There was a finality in my voice that belied the sick feeling of anxiety I always had when I knew that, however much I argued and tried to reason with Joe, I would end up doing whatever pointless, stressful new task he'd thought up for me to do. 'I've done everything you've asked,' I told him, 'including things I never thought I'd ever do, for any reason. I did them to prove I love you, Joe. But I've done enough now.'

An hour later, as the shops were closing, I was still running around Rome looking for the last three 'meaningful' presents, without which I knew the seven I'd already bought would be negated, and Joe would go crazy. I can't remember them all now; I know one was a beautiful hand-cut crystal whisky glass, another a notebook bound in soft Italian leather, and another a very expensive bottle of wine. By the time I returned to the café, where Joe was sitting reading his book and drinking a glass of chilled beer, I still only had eight – and, as expected, he was cruelly scathing.

'You disappoint me once again, Alice,' he told me, after he'd unwrapped all the gifts I'd bought him. 'You have absolutely no originality. Even someone who didn't know me at all could have done better than this.'

At our hotel that night his criticism turned to violence, and by the following morning I'd had enough. Smashing a glass against the side of the bath, I screamed at Joe that I was going to slash my wrists and kill myself. But he just shrugged and turned away, and I didn't do it, of course, although I spent the rest of the day wishing I had.

That evening we went to a bar in a narrow cobbled street a short walk from the centre of the city, which was full of local people, many of them clustered around the bar itself and all apparently talking at the same time. It was quite a small room, decorated with old photographs that seemed to have been hung at random angles on walls that had once been white but were now stained yellow by all the cigarettes that had been smoked there over the years.

Joe and I sat at an old wooden table covered with a white paper tablecloth and ate our meal in relative peace, with remarkably few references to the past. Until that evening, every moment we'd spent in Rome had been miserable. But as I glanced across the table at Joe that evening, I was struck by how relaxed he looked and how different his eyes were in the absence of the dark anger that normally suffused them.

I was still watching him when he turned and took a pen out of the pocket of his jacket, which was hanging on the back of his chair, then reached across the table and started writing something on the tablecloth. When I asked him what he was doing, he paused for a moment, looked at me and smiled – and, suddenly, there he was, the Joe I had fallen in love with.

'Shhh,' he said gently, writing another upside-down letter on the tablecloth, so that it was legible from my side of the table. 'Just watch and read.'

As the letters slowly took shape, I was able to make out the words, 'WILL YOU M'.

When I looked up again, I noticed that some of the people at the tables closest to ours were watching the words form too. Surely, after all the weeks of abuse and incrimination, he couldn't be asking me the question they, also, clearly thought he was going to ask. But a few seconds later, there it was, written in bold capital letters: 'WILL YOU MARRY ME? XX'

Had he done the same thing two or three months earlier, Joe's proposal would have been as unequivocally perfect as everything else about our relationship seemed to be. I could hear the people around us murmuring their romantic approval and suddenly, despite everything that had happened during the last few weeks to turn the dream into a nightmare, I was completely caught up in the excitement of the moment. When I looked across the table at Joe's smiling, handsome face, I knew with absolute certainty that this was the man I loved, the man I wanted to spend the rest of my life with, whose wife I wanted to be, and whose children I wanted to bear.

'Oh, yes, Joe,' I said. 'Of course I'll marry you. I adore you.' And, for once, the tears I wiped from my cheeks were tears of happiness.

'I adore you too, Alice.' Joe smiled and took my hand. 'You are the love of my life. I knew from the moment we met that you were the perfect woman for me. That's why I reacted the way I did.'

'I know. I'm so sorry, Joe. You know I am. And you know how much I love you.'

I hardly dared to believe it was over, and that I'd been wrong to begin to doubt whether the real Joe would ever return. After weeks of unremitting misery, I *had* managed to fix what I had broken, although the happiness I felt that evening was still tinged with guilt for having made him so ill.

When we left the bar around midnight that evening, full of drinks bought for us by other customers and by the beaming bar owner himself – '*complimenti della casa!*' – and with the sound of good wishes for our future happiness ringing in our ears, the paper tablecloth was neatly folded under my arm and I knew that Joe had chosen the perfect place to propose. Three hours later I was sitting on the floor in our hotel room, clutching the tablecloth to my chest, while Joe towered above me, shouting questions about the past and accusing me of having smiled flirtatiously at some man in the bar I couldn't even recognise from his description and wouldn't have noticed anyway, on the night when the man I truly loved had asked me to marry him.

Chapter 9

Joe often said I didn't know him at all, and I suppose he was right. In the early days of our relationship, when everything was still perfect – or, at least, appeared to be – he told me about a brief fling he'd had with a young student, not long before I met him. Then one day, five or six months after the discovery, he said she'd been in contact with him again and that, 'If you love me, you'll let me spend a night with her.'

For someone as moralistic as Joe was, it seemed to be a particularly bizarre request and, despite everything, I was as upset as I imagine he expected me to be. 'I don't know how you could even suggest it,' I told him. To which he replied, simply, 'If you *know* me, Alice, you'll let me do this.'

I continued to refuse to agree to what he was suggesting, until he eventually wore me down, as he always did about everything, by harassing me for days, both verbally and physically, and by threatening to kill himself when I said I couldn't take it any more and was going to leave.

The plan, as Joe explained it, was that I would spend the night in a hotel while the student was at the house, sleeping with him in what should have been 'our bed', although the last bit was never mentioned in so many words.

When the evening arrived, I kept asking Joe, 'Am I going to this hotel or not?' But he wouldn't say, until about ten o'clock, when he finally told me, 'She never was coming, Alice. You should have known I wouldn't do that. I suppose the fact that you were prepared to agree to it just goes to prove that you don't know me at all.'

There were many reasons apart from the constant questioning and violence why the time I spent with Joe was miserable and exhausting. Except on the days when he went to work – which were increasingly few and far between as the weeks went by – I had very little time alone, to think my own thoughts. I couldn't spend more than a minute or two in the shower without him becoming angry and impatient, and he was often in the bathroom anyway, shouting questions at me above the sound of the water.

We both lost a lot of weight during those months too, because neither of us had much of an appetite, and because Joe always stood in the kitchen while I was cooking, demanding clarification of the insignificant minutiae of my past life. Sometimes we managed to eat whatever it was I'd made, and sometimes the violence began before I'd finished cooking it, so that it ended up burned and unappetising. Eventually, when he started snatching sharp knives out of the knife block on the work surface and threatening to kill himself, I became afraid of doing anything in the kitchen at all, and would often slip knives surreptitiously into drawers or the dishwasher while he was talking.

And it wasn't just me that was being worn down by it all. It must have been four or five months after the discovery when Joe sent me home to Devon for the first time – because I'd made him so ill he needed to be on his own for a while, he said. But I didn't want to go home. One reason for my reluctance was that my mother, particularly, still made it clear, on the rare occasions when I spoke to her on the phone, that she disapproved very strongly of my affair with Anthony and that she was deeply disappointed in me. Another reason was that, despite my wretched, bullied existence with Joe, I still wanted to be with him, and I was afraid that if I did leave he might never let me go back or, even worse, might do what he so often threatened to do and kill himself.

I felt responsible for Joe, and, as deranged as it may sound, I did really love him. So the thought that he might kill himself made me incredibly anxious. I don't know if he ever had any real intention of doing it; quite possibly not. But it wasn't a risk I was willing to take, which was one of the main reasons why I didn't ever do, or refuse to do, anything that might push him over the edge so that he carried out his threat. And why, when he told me, at nine o'clock one evening, that he wanted me to go home, I went with him to the station, where he stood on the platform until my train pulled out.

Although he'd said he needed a break from me, it can't have been more than five minutes before my phone rang.

'Tell the people in the seats around you what you are, Alice,' he demanded. 'Are there children in the carriage? How do you think their parents will feel when they know that they're sharing the carriage with a whore? Tell them, Alice. Do it.'

'No, Joe,' I whispered. 'I'm not going to tell them. I'm tired, and so are you. We can talk later. Just leave it, Joe. Please.'

But Joe could never 'leave it', however ill his self-imposed role as interrogator made him feel, and he kept on phoning me for the next hour or more, insisting that I did what he was telling me to do and humiliate myself in a carriage full of people. I suppose that's what brainwashing is, being told something over and over again until eventually all you care about is that the telling stops. So, in the end, I did shout out that I was a whore, but I did it in the space between two carriages, where the toilet is, and out of an open window, so that my voice was snatched away by the wind.

I'd been on the train for about an hour and a half when Joe phoned again and told me he'd changed his mind. 'I want you to come back,' he said. 'Get off at the next stop and catch the first train back to London.' I didn't argue; I didn't even think about saying no. I just crossed the platform at the next station and waited for a train to London.

It must have been about four o'clock in the morning when a taxi dropped me outside Joe's house. It wasn't until days later, when the same thing had happened several times, that I realised he didn't ever intend me to get all the way home. Making me get on the train and then get off it again – at not inconsiderable cost each time – was just another way of exerting his control. And on the rare occasions when he did let me get all the way home, I always had to go back to London the next day.

I knew my parents were worried about me, and that they'd also started having concerns about what was actually happening with Joe. But I lied when they asked me direct questions and I always insisted on going back to London when he told me to.

On one of the rare occasions when he did allow me to go all the way home to Devon on the train, he said it was because I'd made him so ill he needed a few days alone to rest. I dreaded the prospect of having to defend myself in the face of my mother's disapproval. And the reality turned out to be every bit as bad as I'd thought it would be, with Mum taking over Joe's role of inquisitor almost as soon as I walked through the front door, although in her case it was prompted by disappointment in me, rather than aggression.

'Why did you do it, Alice?' she kept asking me. 'You weren't brought up to behave like that. I don't think I will ever be able to forgive you. Your father and I just want to know *why*, Alice.' Which made me feel like an adolescent again, sitting on the sofa in the living room while my mother scolded me for something I'd done wrong. In the past, though, they had always been small things – even if they hadn't seemed small to Mum at the time – because I was actually quite a 'good' child and teenager, working hard at school and never getting into any real trouble. I suppose that's what made it even more bemusing to my mother to learn that I'd broken what she considered to be one of the most self-evident of the ten commandments. I told her repeatedly that I was sorry, but she was as impervious to my apologies as Joe was, and instead of saying something kind and understanding, as I longed for her to do, she kept asking me 'Why?' and telling me how disgusted she was with me.

No one else who knew about my heinous crime reacted the way my mother did – except for Joe, of course. My sister, my therapist, my best friend, even my best friend's mother all said they thought Joe was overreacting and that, although what I'd done clearly hadn't been a good idea on any level, we all make mistakes, which we need to learn from and then move on. If only my own mother could have felt the same way, or, if that wasn't possible, at least have realised how desperately I needed her to forgive me. I don't know whether it would have made me feel that I had an alternative to being with Joe, and I would have escaped and gone home. But it might have.

So, although I hated writing the accounts Joe made me write, the fact that I had to do one while I was staying with my parents at least gave me an excuse to shut myself away in my bedroom. I wrote it on my mother's laptop, sitting for hours at a time on the bed I'd slept in as a child, until my eyes ached and I had pins and needles in my feet. By the time I'd finished it, it was thousands of words long – easily half the length of the thesis I'd written for my Masters degree. My mother knocked on the bedroom door several times to ask if I wanted cups of tea and to try to persuade me to stop writing – even she thought what Joe had asked me to do was unreasonable. In fact, she was so worried about it that, on the second day I was there, she phoned my psychiatrist and asked her to talk to me, to try to convince me not to write the account and to discuss with me the possibility that Joe might not be entirely rational.

At first, I said I wouldn't talk to the psychiatrist. But when my mother brought the phone into my bedroom and said, 'It's Dr Warburg. Please speak to her. It's not right what Joe's asking you to do and the way he's treating you, despite what you did. If you won't listen to me, talk to *her*, please, Alice.'

When I took the phone she was holding out to me, I heard a familiar voice say, 'Hello, Alice. It's Dr Warburg. Your mum has told me what's happened. She's very worried about you. And I am too. I spoke to Paula, after she'd seen you and Joe together a few weeks ago, and she said she hadn't ever seen anything like Joe's reaction. She was very concerned about it – for your sake – and about his constant questioning. And now this – writing accounts of every minute detail of your past. It isn't normal behaviour, Alice. But I think you know that. On some level at least. It's emotionally abusive and controlling. You don't deserve what he's doing to you and you have to say no to him. If you write this absurd account, my worry is that he won't stop at that. There'll soon be something else he wants you to do. Something even more bizarre and unreasonable. And when you've done that, there'll be something else. You have to take a stand now and not let him control your life.'

I wonder what Dr Warburg would have said if she'd known then about some of the bizarre and unreasonable things Joe was already making me do.

I didn't take her advice, of course – obviously Joe wasn't the only one who had lost his sense of reason. I told her I'd think about what she'd said, and then I stayed up late into the night, long after my parents had gone to bed, tapping away on the laptop, so that I could meet the deadline Joe had set me of midnight on that second night.

'My darling Joe,' I wrote in the last paragraph of my mini-thesis, 'I am so very sorry for what I have done to you.' Then I pulled my cardigan more tightly around me and tried to block out the very frightening thought that perhaps everyone else was right and not even this would fix Joe. Maybe there was nothing I could do that would make him well again. But I had to try.

It was on one of the occasions when I'd stayed overnight with my parents and was on a train bound for London the next morning that my phone rang. I assumed without looking at the screen that it was Joe, because it was always Joe, now that almost all my friends had given up trying to contact me, having been brushed off once too often with some lame excuse. This time, though, it wasn't Joe; it was my best friend, Sarah.

I hesitated for a moment before answering the phone. I knew that, after she'd failed to condemn me for having an affair with Anthony, Joe didn't want me to have any contact with Sarah – or with anyone else. But I longed to hear a friendly voice, and almost burst into tears when she said, 'Hi, Alice. It's been weeks since I last saw you. I phoned your mum and she said you were on your way back to London on the train. Which is great, because my mum's in town and we thought it would be nice to meet up.'

'Oh, well, I … It isn't really a good time, I'm afraid.' I was fond of Sarah's mother, who had always been very good to me, and in any normal circumstances I would have leaped at the chance of seeing them both. But I wasn't living in 'normal circumstances' any more and Sarah's suggestion made me anxious.

'We're just round the corner from the station,' she persisted. 'We can meet you there when your train gets in. Just for ten minutes, if you haven't got much time. For a coffee.'

Sarah had been my best friend for years. We'd always confided in each other about the things that mattered to us, and she knew I wasn't the evil person Joe believed – and had almost made me believe – I was. At that moment, more than at any other time in my life, I needed to talk to her. So I agreed.

As soon as I hung up, Joe rang, wanting to know who I'd been talking to.

'Why would you agree to that, Alice?' he asked me coldly when I told him. 'What's wrong with you? Do you ever keep your word about anything? Or are you completely untrustworthy?'

'It's just a cup of coffee with a friend,' I said. 'What could possibly …'

'Have you forgotten what I said, Alice? That you must do everything you say you'll do. No changing your mind about something, or doing anything without telling me.

Have you forgotten about our rules? You've broken my trust, Alice. If there's going to be any chance of rebuilding it, you *must* stick to your word now.'

'I don't understand why agreeing to meet my best friend for ten minutes can be construed as untrustworthy,' I retorted. '*Why* don't you want me to meet her?'

If I hadn't been so weary of going round and round in pointless, never-ending circles, I would have been angry with Joe at that moment. But his voice was calm and he spoke very slowly, as if explaining something to an apparently slow-witted child, as he told me, 'The reason it shows that you're untrustworthy, Alice, is because you promised you wouldn't do anything – and that includes *agreeing* to do anything – without telling me first. And now you've broken that promise. So how am I ever going to be able to trust you?'

Joe had driven to the station to meet me and was waiting at the ticket barrier when I got off the train. And when Sarah phoned me, about ten minutes after the time we'd arranged to meet, he told me to answer it. 'She's not going to stop calling unless you do,' he said. 'But if you want *us* to work, Alice, you won't go and meet her. You'll get rid of her – quickly.'

Obviously it didn't matter if I lied to my best friend, or to my sister or parents, I thought. It was just telling lies to Joe that was dishonest. 'I'm sorry,' I told Sarah, hating myself for being such a coward. 'I'm not going to be able to meet up after all. I'm with Joe. I'm sorry to cancel at the last minute. Say hi to your mum for me.'

'What you mean is that he won't *let* you come and meet us. Isn't that right? Be honest with me, Alice.' Sarah waited for me to answer, but when I didn't say anything she continued, 'We're really worried about you, you know. Oh, wait a minute … Mum wants a word.' And before I could stop her she put her mum, Livia, on the line.

I remember Sarah telling me once that, before she met Sarah's father, Livia had been married, briefly, to a man who was very controlling. I suppose that's why she'd been one of the first people to suspect what might be going on between me and Joe, and why I could hear genuine concern in her voice when she said, 'Joe isn't acting normally, Alice. Have you asked yourself *why* he isn't allowing you to see us? Please come. Just for ten minutes. We really care you about. You know that. I've known you all your life, Alice, and I know you're a good person. You don't deserve to be with someone who wants to control and manipulate you. No one deserves that.'

The whole time Livia was talking to me, Joe was mouthing at me, with increasing impatience. 'Get rid of them,' he hissed at last. 'Just hang up, now. I want to go home. Now, Alice!'

But I didn't do it 'now'. I waited until Sarah's mum had finished telling me, 'It's only going to get worse, Alice;

not better. Believe me. You've got to get out. Please, let us help you.' If only they'd suddenly appear on the road in front of me, I thought. If only Livia could talk to Joe, she might be able to make him realise he's being unreasonable. And if that didn't work, maybe they could drag me away with them, so that I didn't have to make the decision about whether to stay with him or go.

'I'm sorry,' I told her. 'I just can't meet you now.' Then I hung up the phone, and Joe sighed as he asked me, 'How am I ever going to be able to trust you now, Alice?'

I don't know why I didn't do the sensible thing and tell Joe I was going to meet my friend and her mother. He might have shouted at me, but he wouldn't have attacked me physically while we were in the station. And even if he had done, there were plenty of people around who I could have asked for help. Perhaps the reason I didn't do what I wanted to do was some misguided sense of loyalty to Joe, or because I was afraid of losing him altogether if I attempted to break the psychological hold he had over me. Or maybe I was so worn down by lack of sleep and by constantly having to account for almost everything I'd ever done during my adult life before I met him that I was simply no longer capable of independent thought or action.

Whatever the real reason was, I returned to Joe's house with him, to be questioned and accused for the rest of the day and most of the night, and then to be woken up the next morning, after just a few hours' sleep, by him saying, 'That blue skirt you mentioned yesterday, I need to know ...'

It didn't matter if I woke up urgently needing to go to the loo, I always had to answer Joe's questions first.

Chapter 10

As well as sending me almost-home on the train at least three or four times a month, Joe often decided quite late in the evening that he couldn't 'take it any more', and sent me to a hotel for the night. It seemed that, as long as I was with him, he wasn't able to divert himself from his self-imposed, and ultimately pointless, task of discovering the truth. So when the anger, vomiting, dry retching and lack of sleep became too much for him to bear, he would tell me to phone for a taxi and go.

'Just stay in a hotel for one night,' he said the first time. 'I need a break. We both do.' Six months later, I'd stayed in the same hotel on at least forty different occasions, for at least part of the night, and Joe had long since stopped pretending that my doing so was for the benefit of 'us'.

It was quite often one or two o'clock in the morning when Joe told me to leave, but whatever time it was, I always had to be back by 7 a.m., at the latest. Fortunately, the hotel was just a short taxi ride from the house. But it was expensive – particularly as I turned up every time without booking – and, on top of all the holidays and gifts I was buying for Joe, it was yet another cost that helped to deplete my rapidly dwindling savings.

I can remember the first time it happened how relieved I felt as I climbed into a taxi outside Joe's house and closed the door behind me. Although there was always the worry at the back of my mind that he might hurt himself, it was far outweighed on that occasion by the prospect of spending a few hours asleep in a bed on my own, without anyone hurting me or demanding answers to unanswerable questions.

I wasn't allowed to go anywhere or see anyone without Joe's permission, not even my family or closest friends. So, except for the nights I spent travelling almost home on the train and then back to London, or the very rare occasions when I actually got all the way and slept for a few hours in my bedroom at my parents' house, I was with him all the time. A few weeks earlier, that might have seemed like a dream come true. By now, though, I felt as though I was living in a nightmare. But as the taxi sped through the empty streets that first time, I knew that every turn of its wheels was taking me closer to the two things I craved more than anything else: peace and an empty bed.

When I arrived at the hotel Joe had stipulated and walked through the rotating doors into its spacious, high-ceilinged reception area, the night porter nodded and said 'Good evening'. That night I was just like any other weary traveller, albeit one with just a handbag and no luggage. It did strike me later, though, when I'd arrived in the middle of the night on numerous other occasions, that the hotel staff who recognised me might wonder why I was there. But I decided they must get so used to guests checking in at all hours of the day and night, in all sorts of circumstances, that they probably didn't think about it at all – until the night Joe decided to humiliate me there.

The questions had continued until the moment the taxi arrived at the house at about 1 a.m. on a Thursday morning, and I was very tired as I checked in to the hotel a few minutes later, opened my purse to take out my debit card and saw that it wasn't there. I'm not the sort of person who loses or misplaces things – I'd certainly never lost my bank card before – and I could feel panic expanding inside me as I searched frantically through my handbag. The man at the reception desk had that ability some people have of being able simultaneously to convey polite concern and complete indifference and, feeling embarrassed, I moved away from the desk, sat down in a chair next to a tree-sized potted plant and tipped the contents of my handbag on to the table in front of me. But the card wasn't there. Did I leave the card at the house? I wondered. Or maybe it fell out of my purse when I paid the taxi driver. Neither explanation seemed very likely, in view of how careful I always was, but *something* had happened to it.

I was so tired I couldn't think straight. And then it struck me that I'd have to tell Joe when he phoned – as he always did, because despite telling me that he sent me to the hotel when he needed a break from me, he still called me incessantly throughout the night. I began to look again in all the places I'd already searched, as if I thought the card might have miraculously reappeared, and when I opened my purse I realised that, not only did I not have enough cash to pay for the hotel, I didn't even have enough for a taxi back to Joe's house – which, at that moment, was the last place in the world I wanted to go.

Would the hotel staff let me sit in the lobby for what remained of the night, I wondered, or would I be embarrassed further by being asked to leave? If they did let me stay there, maybe I could walk back to Joe's the next morning, or maybe he'd pick me up on his way to work and I could drive his car back to his house after I'd dropped him off. I could have phoned a friend and asked for help. That would have been the sensible, logical thing to do, particularly when I knew that Sarah, or any of the other people I used to be close to, would have gone out of her way to help me. But I don't think the idea even entered my head.

I was running my fingers along the lining of my handbag, hoping there might be a gap in one of the seams that it had slipped through, when I heard someone say, 'Is this what you're looking for?'

At first, my brain wouldn't process the fact that the man standing beside me when I looked up was Joe, and for a moment, as he walked around the table and sat down opposite me, I just stared at him, blankly.

'Where did you get it from?' I asked at last. 'I … I don't understand. What are you doing here?'

'I took it out of your purse,' Joe said calmly.

What I wanted to shout at him was, 'Oh God, Joe, not another of your stupid, pointless, abusive games.' But showing him I was angry would have been even more stupid and pointless, particularly in a public place, where I was the only one of the two of us who'd feel humiliated if he started shouting at me. So all I said was, 'Why? Give it to me, Joe. Please.' To which he responded by leaning forward, across the table, holding my bank card just a few inches in front of my face, and snapping it in two.

'What have you done?' I gasped. 'That's the only card I've got, and you know I don't have any cash. What am I meant to do now? It'll take days for me to get a new card.'

I wasn't trapped physically by Joe, just psychologically, for whatever reason. So there was no logic behind the thought I had then, which was that, without a bank card, I no longer had any chance of escaping if I needed to. Joe must have been able to see that I was beginning to panic, but he just smiled, without humour or affection, and said, 'Do you want to come back home with me?'

'No,' I wanted to scream at him. 'I don't want to go anywhere with you, because I know what will happen when we get there, and I *need* to sleep. Even if it's just for a few hours, I need to be alone in a hotel room, where I can feel safe.' But before I had time to say anything at all, Joe asked, 'You didn't come to this hotel chain with him, did you?' It was a question he'd asked me a thousand times before, the answer to which he didn't seem able to accept.

'No, Joe,' I sighed. 'No, I've told you the names of all the hotels I stayed at with him – long before I met you. I wrote them all down for you, with a list of all the other hotels in the same chains. You know this isn't one of them. That's why you've let me stay here before.'

I made a huge effort to sound calm and reasonable, in the hope that he'd stay the same way – or at least that he'd remain calm, as he was rarely reasonable. But it was too late, and his voice was loud and angry as he told me, 'You're no better than a whore. You know that, don't you? Only a whore frequents hotels with a married man. Only an amoral person has sex with a man who has children.'

'Please, Joe. I'm sorry,' I whispered. 'Please stop. Those children can hear you.' I nodded towards to the reception desk, where a woman with two small, very tired-looking children was checking in. But, clearly, Joe didn't care about *those* children, and he continued to swear at me and call me names. I felt terrible, even more for the children than for myself, because although it crushed another bit of my soul every time Joe verbally abused me, at least I was used to it, almost.

When I stood up and started to walk away, he grabbed my arm and asked, loudly, 'What's the problem, Alice? You didn't mind screwing around with a man who had children. So don't pretend you give a fuck about anyone's kids. People need to know that you're a whore and a bitch. Don't you think so, Alice?'

I was crying by the time he finished his tirade, because I wanted to sleep and because I was weary of being shamed and debased. The questions Joe was asking me now were rhetorical – he wasn't really expecting me to answer them – so it didn't matter to him that I couldn't catch my breath as he continued to work himself up into a state of disgusted fury, until he was shouting, 'You're a useless piece of shit, Alice. Tell me again why you're like a prostitute.'

'Please, Joe,' I whispered again, glancing towards the woman who was standing at the reception desk with a protective arm around the shoulders of each of her children. 'Please don't make me do this. Not now, Joe. Not here. Please.'

I knew as I pleaded with him that there was nothing I could do to divert the inexorable course of his anger. After all, humiliating me was the whole point of what he was doing, although I don't know if he was conscious of that at the time. He certainly didn't seem to be bothered by the fact that the inevitable side-effect of degrading me was embarrassing himself. What was odd too, although I didn't think about it until much later, was that every time he harangued me in public he was running the risk of being seen by someone he knew or at least might recognise him.

'Tell me, Alice,' he said now, his voice rising in pitch as well as volume. 'Tell me why you're like a prostitute or I'll make sure that everyone in the hotel can hear me.'

'Because prostitutes do amoral things and I did amoral things,' I mumbled. 'Because prostitutes are emotionally damaged, and so am I. Because prostitutes have sex in hotels with married men, just like I have done.'

'You didn't say it correctly, Alice. I didn't like your tone of voice. It didn't sound as though you meant it.'

'When will you stop this? Please stop, Joe.' I was sobbing as I pleaded with him. 'You know I meant it. You know I'm sorry. If my tone didn't sound right, it's because it's almost two o'clock in the morning and I *need* to sleep. You need to sleep too, Joe. *Please*.'

But he was completely unmoved – as he always was – by my tears and desperation. 'You have no money,' he said, his voice icily controlled again now. 'You have no bank card and nowhere to go, except to come home with me. And if you want to come home with me, Alice, you're going to have to say it correctly. So say it again. And when you've done that, there's something else I want you to do.'

I never understood the transformation that would take place in Joe. As soon as it occurred, I could see it in his body movements, the expression in his eyes and the way he spoke. It was as if a darker version of him took control, a version that was always there in the background, but that some unknown and unknowable trigger would suddenly bring to the fore without any warning – or, at least, with none that I was ever able to detect. I couldn't work out what was going on in his head either. What was it that made him switch so abruptly from a state of such severe distress that he'd be retching and fighting for breath to violence and vindictiveness? I still don't know the answer to that question.

Although I believed for a long time that I was entirely responsible for whatever was wrong with Joe, I realise now that there was something latent within him long before we met, the release of which would sooner or later have been triggered by something I said or did. What I could never come to terms with, however, was the fact that everyone who worked with him or knew him in his professional persona respected him, because not only was he successful in his job, he was also always charming, thoughtful and kind to them – as he had been to me on the day after I'd been trapped in my flat by the rioting in the streets. No one who knew Joe at work would have recognised the man he became whenever his control snapped – if that's really what happened, because I did begin to wonder if the abusive side of his character was actually just as controlled as the respectable, compassionate side.

What *was* indisputable was that Joe was an intelligent man. So why didn't he ever try to rationalise what he was doing, or realise there was no excuse for his behaviour towards me? In my more rational, clear-thinking moments I knew there was no justification for it, that nothing I had done warranted being treated the way he treated me. For some reason, though, I had become brainwashed by him into believing that it was *my* fault that the man I'd loved – still loved, despite everything – had been transformed from the perfect partner into a ranting, vicious opponent.

As we stood in the lobby of the hotel that night, watched warily by the night staff at the reception desk and by the occasional, late-arriving guest, I felt the last remnants of resistance draining out of me, like air escaping from a deflating balloon, as I asked Joe, very quietly, 'What is it you want me to do now?'

There was a nasty, sneering look on his face as he answered, 'After you've explained to me again – as though you mean it this time – why you're like a prostitute, I want you to run naked through the lobby of this hotel and to the car outside, where I'll be waiting to drive you home.'

'I won't do it,' I told him, rallying for a moment and almost hating him for the callousness of his spite.

But half an hour later, worn down by his insistence and light-headed from lack of sleep, I did what Joe had told me to do. Or, at least, I walked from the cloakroom across the lobby in bare feet, clutching the tight bundle of my clothes in my arms and dressed only in my coat, which I kept closed until I reached the revolving door and stepped out into the night, where Joe could see me.

When we got back to Joe's house, he locked me out. It must have been three or four in the morning, I didn't have a debit card or any cash, and, in my mind, I didn't have anywhere else to go. So I'd resigned myself to the fact that I was going to have to sit on the pavement for what was left of the night, in the hope that Joe would eventually relent and let me in, when I suddenly remembered that I hadn't actually closed the account I'd had with a taxi company I'd used a lot for work. I told the man who answered the phone that I'd locked myself out of the house, my boyfriend was away, and I needed a taxi to sit in for the next few hours until he got home. It seemed like a brainwave at the time – one that, in any other circumstances, might have made me feel rather pleased with myself. Unfortunately, though, and less impressively, it didn't even cross my mind to phone a friend.

When the car came, I lay down on the back seat and dozed – between phone calls from Joe. I don't know what the taxi driver must have thought – I was way beyond the point of worrying about it. But he didn't give any sign that he'd thought about it at all, and just sat listening to the radio until Joe said I could go home, at about 6 a.m.

Joe always got what he wanted. That probably sounds like a very feeble excuse for the fact that, ultimately, I always gave in to even the most humiliating and unreasonable of his demands. I can understand why people might think that in some deep, dark part of my psyche there lurks an exhibitionist who actually got a kick out of running naked through the streets of London and being shamed and embarrassed in public. That isn't true, though, as anyone who really knows me could confirm. I know now that the real reason I did those things was because I wasn't in my right mind: I really believed I'd been entirely responsible for breaking Joe, and that I could fix him. It might take months for that to happen, but when it did, he would love me again and we'd have the sort of perfect relationship I hadn't thought was possible until I met him.

The problem is, I expect Joe thought he was sane too and that he was only doing what I'd *made* him do by having an affair with a married man and then lying about it. I suppose the difference is that I just wanted Joe to love me, whereas I think his reasons for behaving the way he did were far more complicated. Perhaps they included the desire to punish *me* for what the woman who'd had an affair with his father had done, when Joe was just a little boy, and for all the unhappiness of his childhood.

Whatever the explanation, it wasn't just in his dealings with me that Joe was used to achieving whatever he set out to achieve. Part of the reason he was so successful at work, for example, was that when he decided what he wanted he charmed people into doing what was required for him to get it. And if that didn't work, he would manipulate, bully, even coerce them.

One morning, after I'd slept for four or five hours at the hotel – interrupted at intervals by Joe's phone calls – I accidentally left behind a locket and chain he'd bought for me before the discovery. Joe insisted on my wearing it all the time, even at night, but I did take it off sometimes, when I slept alone at the hotel, because it often pressed into my collarbone and woke me up.

Within seconds of my arriving back at the house on that particular occasion, Joe noticed I wasn't wearing the locket and went ballistic. He seemed to think I'd had some deceitful reason for removing it, although I think making me wear it all the time was just a control thing, and he didn't actually believe that. He kept asking me why I'd taken it off, and although he isn't the sort of person who believes in fate, he said that if I didn't find it, it would be like a sign that our relationship wasn't going to work.

I knew I must have left the locket and chain on the table beside the bed in the hotel room, and couldn't believe I'd been so stupid. When I phoned the hotel – which I did immediately – nothing had been handed in. So I went back and asked if I could search the room, but still didn't find it. I even spoke to the guy who'd cleaned the room, who suggested it might have got folded up in the sheets when the bed was stripped and gave me the name and phone number of the laundry company. But it hadn't been handed in there either.

I didn't know what else I could do after that, so I went back to Joe's house, where he ranted and raved at me for a while, telling me that if I didn't find the gift he'd given me, everything would be over between us. Eventually, though, he drove me back to the hotel, where I asked to speak to the manager and told him that the items I'd lost were of enormous sentimental value and very special to me, as well as being totally irreplaceable.

In the end, I think it was the fuss I was making rather than any feelings of sympathy that prompted the hotel manager to agree to let Joe speak to the guy who'd cleaned the room – 'In case he's remembered something since this morning,' Joe said, with his brightest, most charming smile.

Joe's attitude as he talked to the man who'd cleaned the room was equally persuasive but otherwise totally different. Without accusing him openly, or even hinting at the fact that he thought the man might be implicated in any way, Joe's underlying threat was only very thinly veiled as he told him how important the locket and chain were to me and how, for that reason, he was going to have to get the police involved.

'I don't really want to do that,' he said, his face as expressionless as his voice. 'I know that no hotel wants police poking around, asking questions and upsetting their guests. And I certainly wouldn't want anyone to lose their job because of it. But I don't see that I have any choice. Unless, of course, the items were to turn up before the end of the day.'

We'd been back at Joe's house for less than an hour when my phone rang. It was the hotel manager, who told me, 'The cleaner had a more thorough search and he's found your locket and chain in the cleaning cupboard.'

Both items were made of quite high-carat gold and could have been sold for a reasonable amount of money, which is why I thought they'd been lost forever. But Joe didn't seem to be surprised at all when I told him they'd turned up. As I say, he was used to getting what he wanted.

Chapter 11

One day, seven or eight months after the discovery, I was standing in the hallway of Joe's house when, in an unguarded moment, I glanced at my reflection in the mirror. I wasn't supposed to look in mirrors. Joe said he found it 'destabilising', ever since he'd seen a photograph I'd sent to Anthony in an email, of me standing in front of one, naked. I'd taken it long before I met Joe, and had been ashamed of it almost immediately, so I don't know why I didn't delete it. But although I knew it was a mistake, it was *my* mistake, from the past, and it had nothing to do with Joe. Apart from anything else, I couldn't understand why he was so masochistic: if our roles had been reversed I wouldn't have wanted to know any of the details of Joe's previous relationships. Obviously he felt differently.

'If it upsets you so much, you shouldn't have read my emails and texts,' I told him one day, when desolation had made me brave. 'They were nothing to do with *us*. I wrote them before I even knew you. You had no right to read them.' But his response was the same as it always was when I tried to argue with him: I had brought the past into our lives and, in doing so, had made every aspect of it his concern.

The result in this particular instance, with regard to the photograph, was that he had forbidden me to look at myself in any mirror. And because I was always very afraid of doing anything that might trigger another horrible, ugly conversation about the past, I did what he told me to do. It didn't stop the questions, though – Joe didn't really need any specific trigger to set him off.

'Why did you send him that photograph, Alice?' he would ask me. 'What were you thinking, sending something like that to a married man? What sort of immoral, unprincipled person does something like that? How many photographs did you send him, Alice? Think carefully before you answer that question, because I *will* discover the truth. And if I find out you've lied to me, I'll kill you.'

Now, months later, I'd looked in the mirror without thinking, and the questions and accusations began again, with Joe suddenly shouting at me, 'It repulses me to think about that photograph. It makes me sick to my stomach when I think that the woman who said she loved me could have done something so depraved.'

'I'm leaving you,' I told him, blurting out the words before I even realised I was going to say them. 'I can't do this, Joe. I've tried. I'm sorry.'

'You can't leave me!' Joe sounded more shocked than angry. 'Not after everything I've gone through for you. You've made me this way, Alice. I wasn't like this when we met. You know that. You said yourself that our relationship was perfect. You've *made* me ill.'

I think he really believed what he was saying. No, I don't *think* he did; I *know* he did. He truly believed that he had been a normal, well-adjusted, sane man until I came into his life, with my lies and deceit and affairs with married men, and transformed him into the violent, controlling, abusive monster he didn't even realise he was.

'It *isn't* my fault,' I told him. 'I haven't done this to you, Joe. I'm sorry I lied. You know I am. You know I've tried to make it up to you in literally thousands of different ways. But nothing I did could ever justify what you're doing to me.'

'It *is* your fault – you know it; even your mother knows it.' For a moment, he looked like a little boy, indignant at having been accused of something he hadn't done. 'But there *is* something you could do, Alice. You did say you'd do anything for me.'

I felt my stomach tighten. What could he possibly have thought up for me to do that I hadn't already done? I'd given up my job, my friends and my family for him; I'd spent most of my savings on holidays and expensive gifts for him; I'd streaked through the night innumerable times and humiliated myself in a hundred other debasing, soul-destroying ways. Surely, if none of those things had provided him with the proof he said he needed of the fact that I loved him, there was nothing else I could do.

I was so used to crying by that time, I didn't even realise I was doing it as I stood in the hallway of Joe's house, with my shoulders hunched and my back to the mirror, waiting for whatever obscene new demand he was going to make of me.

'I want you to cut your hair,' he said at last. 'You told me some time ago that you'd do it if I asked you to. And now I do. I want you to cut it all off.'

I think it had been just a couple of weeks after the discovery that Joe had asked me if I'd be willing to cut off all my hair to prove I loved him. When I'd said yes, I hadn't thought for a moment that he really meant it. It felt as though, all those weeks earlier, Joe had quite deliberately laid a trap, which was now snapping shut around me.

'No. I won't do it,' I said, raising one hand instinctively to touch the long hair I used to be proud of, but that was now usually a tangled mess, because brushing it required more energy than I could muster.

'But you gave me your word, Alice.' As he said this, Joe sat down on the stairs and clasped his hands around his knees. 'Do it and I'll marry you. And then we'll never talk about the past again. I promise.'

For a moment, I tried to imagine what it would be like to be married to the perfect version of Joe, to be free of the past and never have to talk about it again, to wake up happy every morning and make plans for our future together. I would do anything to fix the mess I'd created and claw back what we'd had for those few brief weeks before the discovery. Then the fantasy faded, reality returned and I knew that it would never be over, whatever Joe promised, or even truly believed. There was nothing I could do, no sacrifice I could make, that would be enough.

'No,' I said again, more firmly this time. 'I won't do it, Joe. It's pointless and crazy.'

Three hours later, worn down by his persistence, I stood looking in the bathroom mirror – with Joe's permission this time – at the jagged line of hair that just covered my ears. As he was hacking at it with a pair of nail scissors, Joe had promised it would be the last thing he ever asked me to do. It wasn't, of course, and as soon as he'd finished cutting my hair into an uneven, crazy-looking bob, he said he wanted me to cut it *all* off. I don't know why I even bothered to argue about it. It was only hair after all, and the sooner I did what Joe wanted me to do, the sooner I could go to bed and sleep.

But it was Joe, not me, who picked up the nail scissors and cut the strands of hair that dropped on to my shoulders and from there to the bathroom floor around my feet. As he did it, I closed my eyes and listened to the sound of my own breathing, and to the snip-snipping of the scissors. When I opened my eyes again, I saw the reflection of a woman looking back at me who had soft, spiky hair about an inch long, with patches of bare white scalp showing through it. 'It'll grow back,' I told myself. 'It's only hair. It doesn't matter.' But the tears still fell, because the woman in the mirror looked so vulnerable and because it felt as though Joe had cut away yet another part of what made me recognisable as me.

When he had finished, he put his hand on my shoulder and turned me gently around so that I was facing him. I looked into his eyes, which seemed softer somehow, and held my breath, waiting for him to say something and almost daring to believe that maybe this time it had worked. Now that he'd seen I was willing to subjugate my vanity so utterly pointlessly, simply because he'd asked me to do it, perhaps he had finally accepted the fact that I really did love him.

Then he spoke, and I could almost hear the sound of my delusion shattering like broken glass. 'I've decided that you don't have to shave it *all* off,' he said, as though he was doing me a huge favour. 'You can leave it like this.'

The next day, I went to a hairdresser and asked if she could tidy it up. I told her I'd cut it myself to raise money for a charity. I felt awful telling a lie that made me look good. But what else could I say? That my boyfriend had done it with some nail scissors as a test to prove I loved him more than I'd loved a married man I'd had an affair with before I met him? It seemed like the lesser of two evils to feel guilty about making myself sound like a better person than I actually was, rather than telling the truth and sounding like a crazy person.

I don't know if the hairdresser believed me. There wasn't much she could do about my hair anyway, because of all the bald patches. But she did try, and then told me to come back when it had grown a bit and she'd be able to cut it to the same length all over. In the meantime, I was just going to have to get used to people's surreptitious glances, some of which made me uncomfortable because they were sympathetic – probably because they thought I'd lost my hair as the result of some sort of medical treatment.

It was a few days after Joe cut my hair that I phoned my sister. It was half past one in the morning and I was in a taxi, on the way back to London after yet another aborted train journey that had taken me almost-home. I don't know what was different about that particular night, but for some reason I felt as though I'd reached the absolute limit of my physical and mental endurance.

Lucy's phone rang for a long time – far longer, it seemed to me, than it would take her to wake up and answer it. But I let it go on ringing, closing my eyes as I waited and repeating the words silently in my head, 'Please, Lucy. Please pick up.'

'Alice? What's wrong? What time is it?' It was as if the sound of Lucy's sleepy voice made something tight and anxious inside me snap, and I started to sob. 'He's cut off all my hair,' I told her. 'It's all gone, Lucy.'

'It's okay, Alice.' Her voice suddenly sounded clearer and more alert. 'It's all right. Just tell me where you are.'

'I'm in a taxi, about an hour away from your house. Can I come and stay with you tonight? Please, Lucy. I know it's late but he made me get on another train and then I was nearly home and he told me to get a taxi and go back to London and I was going to do that but I can't do it any more so I told the taxi driver to turn around and go to your house and now ...'

The words tumbled out of me, punctuated only by my sobs, until Lucy cut across them saying, 'Listen to me, Alice. Just tell me where you are. Of course you can stay. I just need to know *exactly* where you are.'

'I don't know exactly,' I said. 'And I can't pay for the taxi. Joe cut up all my cards.'

'It's okay, Alice. It will be all right. I'm not at the house tonight. I'm in a hotel in Leeds, at a conference. Simon's there, though. He'll let you in and he'll pay for the taxi. Don't worry about that; we'll work it out. But you *must* go straight to my house. Promise me that's what you'll do. And Alice, it *will* be okay.'

If You Love Me

'Yes. All right. I'll go to your house. Thank you, Lucy.' And suddenly the nightmare was over. At the back of my mind, I'd known since a couple of weeks after the discovery that it wasn't going to be possible to repair the damage I thought I'd done to Joe. But I'd kept on trying. Now, I didn't have to try any more. I was going home to the family I hadn't seen for weeks, to the people who really did love me. This time, when they asked me about my relationship with Joe and if everything was all right, I'd tell them the truth about the living hell I'd been trapped in since they last saw me.

As the taxi sped along the dark, almost deserted motorway, the driver listened to the music that was playing softly on his radio and I sat in the back, thankful that he didn't want to chat, and tried to imagine my life without Joe. I hadn't spoken to him on the phone for more than an hour by that time. He'd rung several times while I was on the train, as he always did, but for once I'd refused to humiliate myself in front of the other passengers, as he always made me do. Although I did get off the train when he told me to, it was when I was sitting in the taxi on the way back to London, with no money, no credit cards, and no hair, that I had finally decided I'd had enough.

Joe phoned a few minutes after I'd spoken to Lucy, and at first he sounded almost conciliatory. 'Come back now, Alice,' he said. 'I'll pay for the taxi. We'll work this out.'

Then the hectoring tone returned as he added, 'You can't leave me now, after all you've done to me.'

'I'm not coming back,' I told him. 'I've phoned my sister and I'm going to her house. I told her you'd cut off all my hair. I've had enough, Joe. I know I've said it before, but this time I mean it. I'm not going to be abused by you any more.' But despite the resolution in my voice, I was already wondering if I really could survive without him. It was like being in the grip of an addiction, when you know the thing you're addicted to is harming you but you just keep telling yourself that, eventually, it will make you feel better.

When I'd rung my sister, I had been less than an hour's drive from her house. After travelling for two hours in the opposite direction, the taxi passed a sign saying 'London 25'. I hated myself for not having the strength to say no to Joe. Simon had phoned my sister an hour or so after she'd told him I was coming to their house, to say I hadn't arrived, and when Lucy phoned me she was crying as she pleaded with me not to go back to Joe. 'Please, Alice,' she begged. 'Can't you see that he's abusing you? Surely you realise that. Please come home. I'll be back tomorrow and then we can work it all out. Please, Alice. I'm really worried about you. If you won't do it for your own sake, do it for mine.' I'd felt guilty when she said that, and had really wanted to change my mind and ask the taxi driver to turn around, again. But it was as if I was sleep-walking, following some predetermined path with my eyes open and my conscious mind shut.

When my phone rang again, a man's voice I didn't recognise said, 'Is that Alice Keale?'

'Yes,' I answered hesitantly. 'Who is this?'

'I'm Detective Inspector Roberts, from the Metropolitan Police.'

For a moment I thought I was going to be sick. In the life I'd been brought up to, a phone call from the police in the middle of the night could mean only one thing – that there had been a tragedy of some sort. And the first possibility that came to my mind that night was that Joe had done what he so often threatened he would do and killed himself.

It was a dread that was quickly dispelled, however, when the police officer continued, 'We've just had phone calls from your sister and your parents. They're all extremely worried about you. They say your boyfriend has been abusing you but that you're in a taxi on your way back to him in London.'

It wasn't Joe's life I was concerned about now, but my own, because I knew he would kill me if the police became involved.

'I *am* on the way back to London,' I said, choking back the tears. 'My boyfriend isn't abusing me, though.' I was ashamed by how easily the lie rolled off my tongue. Lying was what had got me into the situation I was in with Joe, and I hated myself for my dishonesty and stupidity. So it was ironic that it was, in effect, Joe who was making me lie again now, so that no one discovered the truth about the life I was really leading with him.

'That's not what your family say.' The police officer sounded stern. 'They say he cut off all your hair and destroyed your bank card, and that the reason you're in a taxi now, in the middle of the night, is because he sent you home on the train, then changed his mind and insisted on you coming back to London.'

'No, they've got that wrong,' I said, as glibly as any Judas might have done. '*I* cut my hair off. I just wanted a change. And I lost my bank card. Neither of those things has anything to do with my boyfriend. We had an argument, that's all, because I was unfaithful. But we're working it out. I'm sorry I worried my family. I was just a bit upset. And I'm really sorry they called the police and that I've wasted your time.'

'We're going to need to see you in person.' The police officer's tone was even sterner. 'We'll come to your boyfriend's house now.'

'No!' Even to my ears, the vehemence with which I said it made the word sound overly defensive. 'I mean … why would you need to see me? I'm fine, honestly.'

'When there's been a report of domestic abuse, we have to see the individual in person. It's standard procedure.' It was clear that he wasn't going to back down.

'Well … actually … I'm not going to my boyfriend's house now. I'm going to a hotel for the night, or for what's left of it. To give us both some space. Can I see you in the morning instead? I'm really tired.' Even as I was speaking, I was wondering why I didn't just tell him the truth. I was being offered the chance to be rescued from the miserable trap I'd fallen into in the name of love. So why did I persist in lying to try to protect Joe?

One way or another, he had taken everything from me, including my money, my job and my self-respect. Now all I had to do was tell the policeman that I *did* need help and then he – and my family – would make sure I was safe. What was wrong with me? Not telling Joe the truth about Anthony had ruined what might otherwise have been a perfect relationship – or so I believed at the time. What terrible mental affliction was I suffering from that prevented me from being honest *this* time, when the impact on my life might be even greater?

'Okay, we can see you in the morning, if that's what you really want. But you must go to your local police station by 11 a.m. so that one of the officers there can confirm you're all right.'

'Of course,' I said. 'Thank you. I'm sorry I've caused all this trouble and wasted your time.'

I had actually been intending to go to Joe's house that night, despite what I'd told the police officer. But when Joe phoned just a few minutes later and I told him what had happened – as I thought I had to do – he said I was making him ill and I should go to the hotel, but be back at his place by 7 a.m.

It wasn't until we were sitting in his car outside the police station at 10.30 the next morning that he finally calmed down enough to stop shouting at me.

'Let's go over it one more time,' he said, his voice quiet now, although still tight and strained. 'What are you going to say to the police officer?'

'I *know* what to say,' I replied. 'We've been over it a hundred times. I just want to go in now, Joe, and get it over with.'

'But you must get it right, Alice. You've made one mistake that has caused a great deal of trouble. You wouldn't want to make another and cause more, would you? So ... let's go over it one more time.'

As I glanced across the road at the police station, the automatic doors slid open and a young couple came out. They were holding hands, and when the girl turned to say something to the boy he smiled and kissed her.

'All right,' I said, sighing as *I* turned to speak to Joe. 'Let's go over it again.'

After I'd reported to the police station, I phoned my sister and told her what I had told the police officer, that Joe and I had had a silly squabble and that I was fine. I know she didn't believe me, and that my mum didn't either when I spoke to her later. But what could they do? As the police must have explained to them, I was an adult and they couldn't force me to accept their help.

Chapter 12

In the spring, Joe and I went on another holiday. To Peru this time, to trek part of the Inca trail. It was a holiday Joe could easily have afforded, but I paid for it all, out of what remained of my savings. And, in any other circumstances, it would have been worth paying almost any amount of money to be able to trek through that amazing landscape of lush valleys and high plateaux, surrounded by spectacular mountain scenery.

Our guide usually walked some distance ahead of us, mostly out of earshot of the endless questions and recriminations that, for me, made walking far more tiring than it would otherwise have been. 'Many people would give anything to do what we're doing,' I thought, as I trudged along the trail beside Joe on what was probably the fourth day, barely noticing the breathtaking beauty of the mountains whose peaks seemed to touch the brilliant blue sky. Then, suddenly, Joe stopped, looked up at the birds that were swooping and calling to each other above our heads and said, 'I think those are condors.'

It was a simple statement, the sort of thing anyone might have said at the time. But the fact that it was said by Joe was extraordinary. I looked at him as closely as I dared, trying to read the expression on his face, and could feel my chest tighten as I realised that the man I was looking at was the Joe I had fallen in love with, what seemed like a whole life-time ago. He must have sensed that I was watching him, and when he turned to look at me he smiled and his face relaxed and was handsome again, the way it was in the photographs I'd taken of him on our first holiday together in Berlin.

For a few minutes I was almost afraid to breathe, in case I broke the spell of the moment and sent us plummeting back into the misery in which we'd spent almost every waking minute of every hour since the discovery. But Joe continued to smile, and while Joe was smiling, the cross-examination stopped and the world around me came back into focus. Having walked for the last few days with my shoulders hunched and my head bowed under the weight of his aggressive questioning, I suddenly noticed the flowers that littered the path at our feet, the sunlight that was reflected off the mirror-like surfaces of distant rivers and lakes, and the sharp, clear outlines of the soaring mountain peaks.

Having wanted to trek the Inca trail for as long as I could remember, all I'd thought about since the day we'd arrived was catching the flight home, where I could at least feel safe knowing that I was in the same country as my family and friends, rather than alone with Joe 6,000 miles away. Now, though, as Joe talked about the things we used to talk about when we first met – what we were going to do with our lives, where we were going to live, how many children we were going to have – I thought that trekking in Peru had done what I'd been unable to do and had brought the real Joe back.

Although it was Joe who wanted to go to Peru when we did, he'd actually trekked the Inca trail before, twice: once with his wife and once with a girlfriend with whom he'd had a relationship that lasted for more than a year. 'There's this special spot,' he'd told me, 'where the view is magnificent. When we're standing there, I think I'll know if I can forgive you and if we can move on.'

I don't think I really understood what he meant about it being a special spot, but it turned out that there was a particular place on the trail where he'd had some kind of epiphany moment with each of them. He didn't have one with me, however. I knew it was the 'special spot' as soon as I saw it, and it really was beautiful. But although I tried to get him to tell me what he was thinking, he refused to say anything, either way. Then the questioning started again, and I knew it hadn't worked. An hour later he was bent double at the side of the trail, dry retching and trying to catch his breath.

It was weeks after we'd returned from Peru when I first began to wonder if he'd done the same thing with his wife and girlfriend as he was doing with me. Perhaps it was a pattern of behaviour for Joe, I thought, believing he'd found the perfect woman and then everything spiralling out of control when he discovered she was only human after all. At the time I just felt disappointed, because being in what must be one of the most beautiful mountain regions in the world had failed to solve the problem – which was beginning to seem insoluble.

Not long after we came back from Peru, I had to have an operation. I'd been experiencing pain in my pelvis for some time, while my stomach was often tender and swollen, and it had eventually been diagnosed as an ovarian cyst. I was told that they are quite common, and that a lot of women have at least one during their lifetime, although many don't have any noticeable symptoms.

Joe insisted that, in some plague-of-locusts sort of way, the cyst on my ovary was the physical manifestation of my amorality and had started to grow as soon as I began my 'sordid affair with a married man'. It was a belief he attempted to reinforce by citing various philosophers and theologians, and after a while I didn't bother to argue with him, because I knew there was nothing I could say that would change his mind.

Joe came with me to the hospital for my appointment with the consultant, and while we were sitting in the waiting room my sister phoned me. I barely spoke to anyone in my family by that time. Joe had severely restricted my contact with my parents and sister, and always supervised and directed any phone conversations I did have. So I was surprised that he told me to answer it on that occasion.

'Hi, Alice. It's Lucy. I'm outside Joe's house with Mum. Sarah and her boyfriend are here too. We know you're in there and we want to see you. We've driven all this way because we're worried about you. Can you open the door and let us in. Please.'

'You're outside the house?' It took me a moment to understand what my sister was saying. 'But I'm not there, Lucy. I've got a hospital appointment. I'm at the hospital.'

'We *know* you're there,' Lucy persisted. 'Your curtains are drawn. Please, Alice, stop lying to us. We just want to help you. Wait a minute … Sarah wants to speak to you.'

Joe's face had darkened, the way it always did when he had to contain his anger for some reason, and he was hissing into my ear the lies he wanted me to tell my sister. The irony, which was apparent to me even then, was that all the misery of the last few months stemmed from Joe's insistence that I must always tell him the truth, while he himself was a master of deceit and false promises.

If only once he had been kind to me or protected me in some way, maybe the impossible task of trying to fix him might not have been so incredibly wearing. But, even at the hospital, when I was facing the prospect of having to have surgery, he didn't feel one iota of compassion or sympathy for me.

'Tell them you don't want to see them,' he said. 'Tell them that turning up on our doorstep like that, out of the blue, and trying to hijack you is abusive behaviour and that they're making your depression worse. Tell them you're fine and they're just being ridiculous.'

'Alice, it's Sarah.' The sound of my best friend's voice made me want to cry. 'I've been trying to contact you, but Lucy said you were on holiday. She told me what happened before you went away, about the taxi in the middle of the night and how he cut all your hair off. We want to help you. If you're really not in the house, at least meet us somewhere, just for a few minutes, so that we can see for ourselves you're okay. Just five minutes, and then we'll leave you alone. You know you'd do the same for me if our roles were reversed. You know that we all love you, Alice. That's the *only* reason we're here. We don't have any hidden agenda, I promise. We just want to know that you're all right. Please.'

I knew Joe was wrong and that genuine concern rather than any attempt to exert control over me was what had prompted their attempt to see me. And I knew Sarah was telling the truth when she said they only wanted to help me. I hated myself for lying to them and for pushing them away. What was I trying to achieve by denying the fact that Joe was abusing me? Why did I persist in pretending – to my family and friends, and to myself – that I was all right? And why was I cutting off the only people who truly cared about me?

The answer to all those questions was the same: because I believed that doing so would somehow make amends to the man who I knew in my heart was ill and *couldn't* be fixed – certainly not by me. What I didn't realise at the time, however, was that the balance of my mind must have been disturbed to some extent, too, for me to have refused so persistently to give up on him.

'I'm fine, Sarah,' I said at last, clearing my throat to mask the sob that escaped as I spoke. 'Honestly. Don't worry about me. It was a misunderstanding: I cut my own hair. *Of course* Joe didn't do it! I just wanted a change. I'm sorry, but I really am at the hospital. I've got an appointment. So I can't see you now.'

In fact, it ended up being another hour before we were called in to see the consultant, during which time Joe barely paused for breath as he muttered malign accusations about my family and friends, and about how, despite everything I'd done to make him so ill, he was trying to protect me from their abuse.

I had turned my phone to silent after Lucy's call, but I saw the screen light up every time she called again, or sent me a message that went unanswered. 'Ignore them,' Joe said. 'They'll give up eventually and go home. We can stay at a hotel tonight if necessary.' But I couldn't help wishing he was wrong and that my sister and best friend would somehow find out which hospital I was at and the next time the automatic doors slid open I would look up and see them walking towards me.

Joe insisted on my asking the consultant if the cyst could have been caused by sex and how long he thought I'd had it. 'We don't know what causes ovarian cysts,' the consultant said. 'They're very common, and most of them disappear again after a few weeks or months without causing any problems or needing any treatment. But, for reasons that aren't really understood, some continue to grow and can cause symptoms of pelvic pain, bloating, etc., as in your case, or even block the blood supply to the ovaries, which is why I would recommend having it removed. And in answer to your second question, there is no way of knowing how long it's been there.'

Joe knew, though, or thought he did, and while the consultant was showing us the ultrasound scan of the cyst that had grown on my ovary there was an expression of revulsion on his face. He didn't let the consultant see it, of course, and by the time he turned back to look at us Joe was nodding sympathetically again, and said all the right things. Later, as soon as we were alone, he told me that he found my ovarian cyst repulsive and he wanted me to have the operation to remove it as soon as I possibly could.

Of all the countless occasions when I felt miserable and alone, I think it was on that day more than at any other time that I longed for him to say something kind to me. 'Don't worry, Alice,' he might have said. 'I know you're dreading having to have surgery, but you'll feel better after it. And I'll look after you.' Instead, he called it 'biblical retribution' and berated me for the amoral behaviour that no amount of scientific evidence would have convinced him hadn't caused it.

We didn't go home until quite late that evening, when Joe drove slowly past the end of our road, to make sure Lucy and the others had gone, before turning round and parking. I was anxious for the rest of the night, in case they decided to come back, but they didn't, although they did tell me later that they wished they had.

The few weeks I had to wait before I had the operation were a difficult time for me. I'd been having heavy periods for a while and had become a bit anaemic, which was making me very tired. Also I was dreading the thought of Joe being at the hospital with me when the time came. If only I could have my family there, I thought, or a friend like Sarah who would reassure me by telling me, as often as I needed to hear it, that it was straightforward surgery and everything was going to be okay. I wanted to know that I'd wake up from the anaesthetic to smiling faces and friendly voices, not to see Joe waiting impatiently for me to open my eyes so he could tell me again that my condition was the result of divine intervention or karma or whatever type of cosmic justice he might have decided had caused it while I was on the operating table.

As much as I wanted to do so, however, I knew I couldn't tell any of the people who would have looked after me, because they would do the one thing I both wanted and dreaded them doing, which was to insist on visiting me in the hospital. And Joe simply wouldn't have allowed that. I think, in reality, I might have found it difficult too. Because if they *did* come when I was weak and off my guard, I might have broken down and told them the truth about the life I was living with Joe, and then I wouldn't have been able to go on pretending to myself that I could fix him, which would mean that the misery I'd endured for the past few months had all been for nothing.

I was due to have a laparoscopy – keyhole surgery, as it's sometimes called – which involved a relatively mild general anaesthetic and meant I wouldn't have to stay in hospital overnight. Normally, I hate anything to do with hospitals, and being admitted for an operation would have been high on my list of things I never wanted to experience. But I might have been the only person undergoing surgery that day who desperately wanted to stay in overnight. In fact, though, Joe seemed genuinely concerned as he drove me to the hospital that morning. Then the questioning began again, and by the time I was given the anaesthetic injection I didn't care what happened to me.

When I woke up in the recovery room, my first thought was that I didn't want to go back to the day ward, where Joe would be waiting for me. 'He's been really worried,' one of the nurses told me. 'Just pacing up and down the whole time you were in theatre. Poor man.' She was trying to be nice, telling me, in effect, that my boyfriend loved me. But he seemed to have got over his anxiety by the time I did go back down to the ward.

It was another four hours before I was allowed to go home, during which time I was tempted to pretend I felt ill, so that I could stay and get a peaceful night's sleep. In the end, though, Joe was so desperate to take me home that I allowed myself to believe everything would be okay. And in fact he wasn't violent that evening, although he did keep me awake for most of the night with his questions.

Sometimes, on the days when Joe went into work, I would drop him off in the morning and then pick up a latte and an almond croissant from the bakery on my way home. I lived for those moments when I was sitting alone in the living room of Joe's empty, silent house, drinking my coffee and eating my croissant. They only ever lasted for a few minutes – certainly never more than half an hour – before Joe phoned or texted me and I'd start doing the cleaning and whatever other chores had to be completed before he came home.

Every day that Joe went to work I had the same routine. I'd get up when he did, wash with him, make coffee for us both, get dressed when he did, drive him to work, and collect him at the end of the day, or at whatever time he decided he wanted to come home. Sometimes he only went into the office for an hour, and I would have just got back to the house when he'd phone and I'd have to go out again to pick him up. And sometimes he'd make me wait for him, sitting in the car outside his office, listening to the radio and trying not to resent the fact that I had been robbed of a few precious hours of relative peace and quiet, that would only have been interrupted by his regular texts and phone calls.

When Joe wasn't with me I could look at whatever I wanted to look at without being afraid that he'd accuse me of staring at someone in some unacceptable way. I could listen to whatever I wanted to listen to on the radio and not have to worry in case someone said something that, in Joe's mind, had some ridiculously tenuous link to 'the married man'. Essentially, I could pretend that I was living a normal life, in which everything was the way it used to be and nobody asked me to do things that couldn't be done. It was that pretence and those brief periods of time I spent on my own that kept me sane – or, at least, as sane as I was.

It turned out that, by the time my family became aware that something more serious was going on between me and Joe than simply him trying to come to terms with my affair with a married man, he had changed his landline number. So they had no way of contacting me except via my mobile phone, which he monitored very closely. Occasionally, he dictated a text message that was supposed to be from me to my mother or sister, but was usually phrased in a way that didn't sound like me at all. Sometimes the messages would include some critical comment about my mother: that I thought her attitude to my relationship with Anthony was ridiculous, for example, and that this was why I wasn't going home. As outgoing calls on Joe's landline were itemised, and I didn't dare make any phone calls or send any texts on my mobile that he hadn't approved, I couldn't do anything to counteract the impression he was giving to my family. I did sometimes call my sister on a payphone while he was at work, but even then I was cautious about what I told her.

Then one day, when I was so worn down by Joe's abuse that I just wanted *someone* to know what was going on, I phoned Lucy and told her I was going to leave my phone on in my handbag when he got home from work, because I knew it wouldn't be long before he kicked off about something. 'Whatever you hear,' I told her, 'don't call me back. And try not to worry.' It was an awful position to put my sister in, but I was close to being at the end of my tether and I didn't know what else to do.

On that particular occasion Joe started yelling almost as soon as he walked into the house, as he often did. Lucy told me later that she could barely believe what she was hearing and was really frightened for me. She tried to record it, and was furious with herself afterwards because she didn't manage to do so. But she did tell my mother what she'd heard and then phoned my psychiatrist, who advised her to contact the police. And that's why, a couple of days later, after I'd dropped Joe at work and was sitting in the living room, sipping my cup of coffee and listening to the quietness of the house, the doorbell rang.

No one ever called at the house. In fact, the only contact we had with any of the neighbours by that time was when they told us that if they heard me screaming again they were going to phone the police. It was a threat that had been made on two or three occasions, by different neighbours, and it sent Joe into a rage. He was always very polite and charming to the neighbours themselves, of course, apologising for having disturbed them and explaining that I wasn't very well, mentally, and that it was sometimes difficult to contain my 'episodes'. Then, as soon as they'd gone, he would put his hand over my mouth and push me up against the wall, pressing his arm across my throat so that I couldn't breathe as he hissed in my face, 'Are you *trying* to get me into trouble, Alice? Is that why you make all that noise? So that the neighbours will hear you and phone the police?' And I would apologise and deny that it had been my intention, not that it would have mattered anyway, as none of the neighbours had ever knocked on the door when Joe was at work and asked if I was all right.

So my immediate thought that morning was that Joe must have waited for me to drive away from the office and then got a taxi back to the house, in the hope of catching me out doing something I shouldn't be doing – which, in his eyes, would include what I *was* doing, which was basically nothing.

From where I was sitting I could see the front door through the living-room window, and the man and woman who were standing there could see me. So there was no point pretending not to be in, as I would normally have done.

'Are you Alice Keale?' the woman asked as soon as I opened the door.

'Yes.' I raised my eyebrows quizzically.

'We're from the Metropolitan Police,' the woman said. 'The Domestic Abuse Unit. Your family and a friend of yours contacted us. They're all extremely concerned about you and we'd like to have a word. Can we come in?'

Someone once told me that if you ask a question that could equally well have the answer yes or no, you have to be prepared for either response. It was good advice, but I got the impression on this occasion that 'Can we come in?' wasn't really a question at all and that I didn't have much choice. It wasn't police officers themselves I was afraid of, however, but what Joe would say when he found out that they'd been to the house. I'd have to tell him, and when I did he'd go crazy. I could feel my heart racing at the very thought of it.

I knew my family and best friend were worried about me. At times when I felt as though I couldn't take it any more, I'd started to let slip little bits of information to my sister – about Joe cutting my hair, and about him making me take long train rides almost-home, sometimes as often as two or three times a week. My worry now, however, was what they might have told the police.

I led the way into the living room, where the two officers sat on the sofa while I perched on the edge of a chair opposite them.

'People are very worried about you, Alice.' It was the woman speaking again. 'And I have to say, from what your family and friend have told us, I think they have reason to be.'

'I know they've been worried,' I said, trying to sound like someone who's already done something stupid, rather than someone who's about to throw away her one chance of getting the help she needs. 'The truth is, everything's been blown out of proportion. You know what mothers are like. I was emotionally unfaithful to my boyfriend during the first five weeks of our relationship, and when he found out he took it very badly. It's just taking a while for us to work things out. But we're getting there.'

It sounds ridiculous to me now, but I imagine police officers working in a domestic abuse unit had heard it all before – or, at least, variations on the same theme.

'But it's nine months since he found out, isn't it?' Again, it wasn't really a question. 'Don't you think your boyfriend might be overreacting by continuing to make it a bone of contention? I'd have thought that nine months would be more than enough time to work things out, if you're going to be able to do so. Your sister says he cut all your hair off and threw away all your clothes.'

'Clearing my wardrobe' was something Joe had started when, in response to one of his early questions, I'd said that I was wearing jeans on the evening that Anthony and I first had sex. Joe had already thrown out all my underwear, and then specified the style and colour of bras and pants I was to wear in the future. So then he ripped up all my jeans, which I wasn't allowed to replace, or, in fact, wear at all. Next, he made me throw out all the tops I had in certain colours, the dresses I'd worn on particular occasions, and eventually almost every item of clothing I possessed. When everything I'd chosen myself had been got rid of or destroyed, I wore only items of clothing I'd bought under Joe's supervision and direction, none of which bore any resemblance to anything I might have worn at any time during the eighteen months when I was seeing Anthony.

I didn't say any of that to the police officers, of course. Instead, I lied to them, the way I seemed to lie about everything to everyone except Joe by that time, and told them, 'It wasn't my boyfriend who cut off my hair. *I* did it. I wanted a change of style, that's all. He didn't throw out my clothes, either. I did. And he doesn't tell me what to wear. I know he overreacted to what happened, but it was understandable because he felt betrayed and was struggling to come to terms with it all.'

'What do you do during the day?' It was the first time the male police officer had said anything, and his question took me slightly off guard. 'Your mum says he hasn't allowed you to work for several months. That must be very isolating for you. So what do you do every day? How would you say things were between you and your boyfriend? Do the two of you argue a lot? Your sister said she overheard one of your arguments on the phone and that he sounded "dangerous and unhinged". She was very frightened for you. Is your boyfriend violent with you?'

The only question I answered was the last one. 'No, he isn't violent with me,' I lied. 'We do argue a bit, because he's still working it all through. But *of course* he hasn't forbidden me to work. I get depression, which has been made worse by what's happened. That's why I don't work at the moment. I just don't feel up to it right now.'

I had been so programmed by Joe that the explanations and excuses were almost automatic, whereas what I really wanted to say to the police officers was, 'Help me! Please don't leave me here. Take me away with you. Yes, he's dangerous and unhinged; he's violent and irrational too. We argue all the time. I barely sleep or eat. I've lost count of the times he's strangled me and threatened to kill me, and I'm really, really frightened about what he might do to me. Cutting off my hair and throwing out my clothes are only a small part of it. He makes me run naked through the streets at night. He won't let me have any contact with my family or friends. Can't you see that I've been lying to you and that I need help, but that I can't admit it because, despite everything, I think I still love Joe. If you won't take me away with you, at least tell me that he's right, that everything is the way he says it is, and that I haven't endured all this suffering for nothing.'

I wondered later whether, if the police officers had persisted in their questioning, I might have told them any part of the truth – had my phone not rung at that moment.

'I'm sorry,' I told them. 'It's my boyfriend. I've got to take this.' Then, into the phone, 'Hi, Joe. I can't talk right now. The police are here. Can we speak later? Yes, of course. Bye.'

Joe answered very calmly when I told him about the police. But I knew him well enough to be able to sense the seething rage that he was only just managing to control, and to know that I would pay for the police officers' visit when he got home. And still I didn't tell them the truth and ask them to help me.

When they left, they took with them the statement I had signed confirming that everything in my life with Joe was fine and devoid of domestic abuse. They did tell me they didn't believe me, but said they couldn't force me to accept their help if I didn't want it. So they gave me a number to call if I changed my mind.

As soon as they'd gone, I picked up my phone and rang Joe. Although I had hoped he might be in a meeting, so that I'd have some time to collect my thoughts, he answered immediately and said, in a voice cold with anger and distrust, 'I need you to meet me for lunch. Right now.'

Chapter 13

We were in Sardinia, on the last holiday I was going to be able to afford before my savings ran out, and I could hardly believe how well things had been going – 'well' for us, at least. On the third day we were there, there was a period of maybe two hours when Joe didn't ask me a single question about the past.

We had hired a small open boat with an outboard motor to explore the isolated coves and bays along the coast, mooring it offshore so that we could swim in the crystal-clear water. After we'd swum, we would lie on the pebbly beach, letting the warmth of the sun soak into our bones. On this particular day Joe was lying at one end of the boat with his back to me, reading, while I was sitting at the other end, sketching the bay and an old villa that could just be seen among the trees on the cliff above it.

As I sat there, listening to the sound of the birds gliding through the cloudless sky above our heads, I felt almost happy. I rarely daydreamed since the discovery; I was always too anxious, miserable and exhausted to think about anything beyond the confines of my life with Joe. But I found myself wondering what it would be like to live in a house like the one I was drawing, and to wake up every morning to the sound of the waves lapping gently on the shore.

It was late afternoon, but the sun was still very hot, and when I glanced up from my sketchpad I could see that the skin on Joe's back was starting to burn. 'I should tell him,' I thought. 'So that he can put on some more sun cream.' But that would mean breaking the rare tranquillity of the moment and risk setting him off again, demanding answers to his crazy questions and shattering the silence with accusations and abuse.

So I didn't say anything, and it wasn't until we were finishing our dinner in a restaurant that evening that he started again. He wasn't drunk, but he'd been drinking, and alcohol always seemed to make it worse. As soon as he spat the first question at me, I could feel the tears filling my eyes, because I knew I'd been stupid to have allowed myself to hope that night might be different from any other, and because I also knew that, if I gave up hoping, there would be nothing left.

'Why didn't you say something?' Joe asked me angrily.

'What do you mean?' I replied, confused by the question and desperately searching my mind for something that might have triggered it, something I'd done wrong or had failed to anticipate.

'Are you telling me you didn't even notice the family who've just left?' he demanded, nodding his head towards the now empty table next to ours and speaking so loudly that several people at other tables glanced warily in our direction.

'Yes, I … I saw them as we sat down. But what about them?' I whispered. My heart was racing as I tried to remember if I'd looked at them in some unguarded moment in a way that Joe could misinterpret.

This had happened before, in a restaurant in London one night. I hadn't even been consciously aware of any of the people at other tables on that occasion, and Joe hadn't said anything until we got back to the house, when he suddenly lost it and started screaming at me, 'You *know* what you did.'

'I *don't* know, Joe,' I kept telling him. 'I don't know what you're talking about. What did I do?'

'*You* tell *me*,' he'd insisted, grabbing me around the throat and pushing me with such force against the wall that I could almost feel the bruise spreading across my windpipe. 'You tell me what you did wrong. Don't pretend that you don't know.'

But I didn't know what I'd done on that night in London any more than I knew now, in the restaurant in Sardinia, and I was afraid to guess in case I said something that gave him an excuse to blame me for something else too. In the end he told me that, as we walked into the restaurant, I'd looked at the two men sitting at the table next to ours – 'flirtatiously', Joe said. The accusation was ludicrous. If I ever had been prone to looking at men flirtatiously – which I don't believe I was – those days were long gone. In fact, most of the time I barely noticed my surroundings at all, and I certainly hadn't been consciously aware of any of the people sitting at any of the tables in that London restaurant. Maybe I did look in the direction of the two men when we walked in. Or maybe it was all in Joe's imagination. But whatever he believed I had done, I didn't deserve his vicious attack that night, or the bruises and bite marks that were its legacy the next morning.

So now, as we sat in the restaurant in Sardinia, I tried desperately to guess what heinous crime Joe might be accusing me of.

'The girl,' he said at last. 'Don't tell me you didn't notice the girl. She must have been about the same age as the daughter of the married man.'

'I'm sorry,' I stuttered, resisting the sudden urge I felt to lay my head on the table and sob until I fell asleep. 'I should have paid more attention. I didn't notice her. I wish I could take back what I did. You know how sorry I am.'

I hated hearing myself speak in that pathetic, obsequious 'victim's' voice. But it was as if I'd become conditioned to being servile and submissive, accepting blame without question for anything and everything Joe accused me of, however unlikely or absurd it actually was.

'How could you do it? It's disgusting.' He was shouting now. 'You've ruined that girl's life forever. You're a fucking whore.'

In fact, Joe always swore at me when he was angry. He had a way of saying certain words that made them sound particularly harsh and ugly. But I haven't normally included them here, mostly because I find it so upsetting to remember the expression on his face when he said them.

'I'm sorry,' I said again, while silently, in my head, I was pleading with him: 'Please don't do this. I can't take it any more. It's madness. The way you behave is crazy. And I'm crazy too, for trying, over and over again, to find the key that will make everything the way it used to be, when the rational side of me knows that will never happen and I should simply walk away.'

I knew the violence wouldn't start until we were alone in our hotel room, but the verbal abuse was just as damaging in its way.

'How could you do that to a family?' he asked me again. 'You met his daughter and then had an affair with her father. What sort of person does something like that? Tell me, Alice. Really – tell me. I want to know. Because I can't even begin to imagine who would do that to a seventeen-year-old girl. You disgust me. Depression is no excuse. There *is* no excuse.'

By the time he paused for breath, the people who had been glancing in our direction had all turned away and were pretending they couldn't hear him. No one told him to be quiet or asked if I was all right, although it wouldn't have made any difference if they had, because I'd only have said I was fine. What did often surprise me, though, was how averse people were to interfering, even when Joe's tirades quite clearly interrupted their own enjoyment of meals and conversations. The trouble was, the more often Joe ranted in public without anyone intervening, the less likely it became that I would ask a stranger for help, and the more trapped I felt.

Bizarrely, in the circumstances, after we left the restaurant that night we went to a bar. No one intervened there either, even when Joe twisted my arm behind my back, leaving a mark that became a bruise where each of his fingers had dug into my flesh. At least he wouldn't really hurt me while there were other people around. And if we stayed in the bar long enough, he might have calmed down a bit by the time we did go back to the hotel, and then he might fall asleep. He didn't, though; not that night.

As soon as I had closed the door of our hotel room behind us, he grabbed me by the throat and slammed me against the wall. I was sobbing and gasping for breath, but he just tightened his grip and then spat into my face. I still

don't know whether he lost control in those moments –
overcome by whatever mental torment or affliction
fuelled his rage – or whether he always knew exactly what
he was doing. Then, suddenly, he banged my head so hard
against the wall I thought he might have cracked my skull.
I cried out in pain, but that just made him do it again, and
again, until the room was spinning and I thought I was
going to pass out.

'Why are you doing this, Joe?' He had his hand around
my throat and the words were barely audible. 'I love you.
Stop. Please.'

'If you speak again, I'll kill you,' he said, his breath hot
against my cheeks and his eyes full of hatred. 'If you move,
I'll kill you. Do you think I won't do it? Oh, believe me,
Alice, I will. No one knows where you are. I could throw
your body off the back of the boat and no one would ever
find you. Maybe, one day, it would wash up on some distant
shore. But by that time it would have begun to decompose
and be so bloated by seawater you'd be unrecognisable.'

And I *did* believe him. Ten months earlier I'd have
sworn on everything I held dear that Joe wasn't capable of
hurting anyone, let anyone of cold-blooded murder. But
I knew he meant every word of what he said that night,
and I didn't doubt for a moment that he was capable of
doing the things he described. So I didn't try to resist
when he dragged me across the room, pushed me down
on to the bed and then lay beside me, releasing his grip

around my throat as he did so and starting to rap on the side of my head with his knuckles. The pain was excruciating, and I was very afraid that he might kill me with one of his blows, intentionally or otherwise.

'In some countries,' he said, his tone almost conversational now, 'you would be imprisoned, even put to death, for what you've done. In some countries whores are subjected to very strict laws.'

'I'm sorry,' I whispered again, and although I could feel my tears soaking into my hair – the way Joe used to tell me that his mother's did after his father left them – I didn't dare to move. I knew there was nothing I could do or say that would make him stop hitting me: he would stop only when he wanted to, when he was ready to go to sleep. If I did survive the night, I would have to think up excuses to explain to anyone who asked why my body was covered in bruises – the shower head fell on me; I tripped on an uneven pavement; I walked into something when I wasn't looking where I was going. But I was used to telling lies for Joe.

The sun was just starting to rise and I could hear the sound of birdsong when Joe finally fell asleep. 'At least I'm still alive,' I told myself, although, at that moment, I couldn't think of any reason why that was a good thing. Then, despite the terrible, throbbing pain in my head, I slept too.

* * *

Sometimes, instead of threatening *my* life, Joe said he was going to kill himself. I always thought he was bluffing, until one night when I really did believe he was going to do it.

The interrupted train journeys home still happened occasionally, when he suddenly decided I was making him so ill he couldn't take it any more. But it had been a few weeks since he'd last allowed me to get all the way home, arriving late at night and leaving again very early the next morning, despite my parents' pleas to stay or at least to talk to them. I didn't ever talk to my sister or parents on the phone either, except when Joe was there, telling me what to say and how to say it. So, at first, I couldn't understand why he agreed so readily to visit my father's elderly cousin, who was staying with my great-aunt while on holiday from her home in Australia. But then he explained that he wanted my father's cousin to see what a well-adjusted, happy couple we were, so that at least one member of my family would realise that it was my parents and sister who were dysfunctional, insisting that they wanted to see me when all I wanted was to be left alone, with Joe.

I was very fond of my great-aunt and in any normal circumstances would have been looking forward to seeing my father's cousin too. But after a really bad, almost sleepless night of abuse, I woke up on the morning of our proposed visit dreading the thought of having to pretend that everything was fine and that Joe really was the charming, kind, considerate man he appeared to be.

I don't what triggered his meltdown on that particular night. It didn't really make any difference, because even on the occasions when Joe did tell me why he was more than usually upset, the reasons he gave didn't make any sense. That evening, though, it somehow ended up with Joe sitting on the floor in the hallway holding a knife to his neck, while I knelt beside him trying to think of some way of distracting him from doing what he was threatening to do.

He often took a knife out of the wooden block in the kitchen and said he was going to kill himself. Sometimes he would lie in bed with the duvet pulled up to his chin, making stabbing motions against his stomach. This time, though, as he interrogated me about whatever trivial detail he'd decided required further clarification, he kept pressing the tip of the knife against his neck so that it made an indentation on his skin and eventually drew a drop of blood.

'You will stay with me while I die, won't you, Alice?' he pleaded, the cold expression I could see in his eyes seeming to belie the pathos in his voice. 'If you love me, as you say you do, tell me that you'll do this one last thing for me and hold me while I bleed to death.'

It sounds absurdly melodramatic when I describe it now, but at the time my judgement was so skewed by guilt and lack of sleep that I didn't see it clearly for what it was. I did wonder, though, if it was just another form of the control and cruel manipulation that he was so good at and that directed every aspect of my life. But something made me realise, as I knelt on the floor beside him, that I didn't really know him at all, and maybe this time he did really mean it.

'Please stop it, Joe,' I begged him. 'Why are you doing this? I've told you thousands of times that I love you. I've done everything you asked me to do to try to prove it to you. What more ...'

'I've left a note in the drawer of my desk at work,' he said, as if he hadn't heard me. 'And another in the glove compartment in the car. They explain everything. I want my colleagues and my family to know why I'm doing this.' He paused for a moment, holding the knife away from his throat and bending forward slightly as he dry retched, and then, when I shifted my position, he again pressed the blade against his skin.

I didn't know what to say to try to calm him down. He'd already told me several times about the notes, and I'd asked him if I could go and get the one in the car. I wanted to read it myself so that I'd know whether he really was as distraught as he appeared to be, or whether the two hours I'd just spent kneeling on the floor while he prodded and poked at himself with a knife had been a pointless waste of time. But he became so agitated when I suggested it – without telling him the reason, of course –

that I was afraid to risk leaving him on his own, in case he really did hurt or even kill himself.

At one point, when he jabbed the knife against his throat with more force than he'd done before, I screamed, which made him angry.

'Why did you do that, Alice?' he demanded to know. 'Do you want the neighbours to hear you? Is that what you want? The neighbours to come round? Or maybe the police?'

'Yes, that *is* what I want,' I told him. 'Because I don't want you to kill yourself. You need help, Joe. Please, let me go to the neighbours and get help.'

'All you had to do was tell me the truth,' he said, switching the focus, as he always did, away from himself and back to my amoral, repulsive, disgusting behaviour, which had apparently pushed a lovely, sane man over a precipice into a state of cruel, obsessive retribution. 'That really was all you had to do, Alice.'

I didn't know what truth he was talking about. I'd lost track of all the questions he'd asked me that night, questions I'd already answered countless times before, about things that didn't matter anyway.

Suddenly, I felt the urge to shout at him, 'Just do it! If you're going to kill yourself, get it over with. Or put the knife down and go to bed, so that I can sleep too.' But as soon as the thought entered my head, I imagined him lying on the floor with blood dripping from a wound in his neck while I cradled his head on my lap, crying and telling him how much I loved him, as we waited for the ambulance to come and for someone to rescue us both. And although Joe had hurt me a thousand times, biting me, bashing my head on walls and floors until the world around me slipped out of focus, and covering my body with bruises, I couldn't bear the thought of him hurting himself. So I continued to kneel on the floor beside him, until he tired of the melodrama he'd created, stood up, dropped the knife on the kitchen work surface, got into bed and immediately fell asleep.

That was why I was so tired the next morning, as I sat beside Joe in the car, holding the box of expensive cakes he'd bought as a gift for my great-aunt, and opened the glove compartment to look for his note. He hadn't been out to the car on his own that morning, before we came out together, so there was no way he could have removed it. But all I found was an out-of-date parking sticker, some plastic gloves from a petrol station, a biro and a few pound coins.

I don't know why I was surprised that he'd lied about the note. I believed I still loved him, and I certainly didn't want him to harm himself. But I hated the feeling of having been tricked into spending hours sitting on the floor in the hallway, crying and trying desperately to think of something I could say that would prevent him from taking his own life.

Suddenly, he reached across the car and slammed the glove compartment shut, shouting at me as he did so, 'What the hell are you doing? What are you looking for?' And as I sat beside him, not daring to say anything that might antagonise him further, while he continued to harangue me, I couldn't help thinking that only Joe could reinterpret the events of the previous night and somehow make every aspect of what happened my fault.

When we arrived at my great-aunt's house, Joe was charming, amiable and polite, while I tried my best to act the part of his fortunate, loving girlfriend. I don't know if we managed to pull it off, or what my relatives said to each other after we'd gone. I no longer had a reliable yardstick by which to measure reality, so it's possible that what seemed convincing to me didn't fool the people who loved me for a moment.

Chapter 14

Apart from my own psychotherapist and the one Joe found for himself, who we also saw together, there was only one other person I'd talked to about my affair. She wasn't even someone of my own choosing, although I spoke to her just a few days after the discovery, at a time when I still had the capacity, if not the will, to make decisions for myself, theoretically at least. She was a neighbour of Joe's, who he'd apparently known for about ten years but who I'd never previously met.

Joe had insisted on my talking to her, although given his reaction to what he'd just discovered about my relationship with Anthony his explanation seemed paradoxical: 'Helen cheated on her husband with the partner she's with now, who's the father of her child.' He talked about her as though he hadn't judged her at all, which didn't make any sense, although who knows what tangled psychological web was involved in his relationship with her.

'I've told her what you did,' he said. 'And she's agreed to come over for a chat.'

'A chat with *me*?' I was appalled.

'Well … yes.' Joe seemed surprised by my reaction. 'I think that would be a good thing. Don't you?'

I realised later that he didn't actually care whether I thought it would be a good thing or not, but I already knew there was no point in arguing. Although he made it sound as though he'd arranged our bizarre tête-à-tête for *my* sake, so that I could unburden myself to another woman who would have every reason to understand, I think what he was really hoping for was that I would tell Helen things I hadn't told him, and then he would be one step closer to knowing 'the whole truth'. But even by that time there wasn't really any more 'truth' to be told.

When Helen came over one evening, Joe told me to stay in the bedroom while he talked to her first. I'd never met her before and would far rather not have spoken to her about the affair, or about any other aspect of my private life. But that clearly wasn't an option. Everything about Joe's idea was peculiar, including the fact that Helen didn't seem to be surprised to have been asked to get involved. I imagine Joe had spun her a story that made it seem as though *I* was the one who wanted to talk to her, to unburden myself, perhaps, because I didn't have any friends of my own to confide in.

Eventually, Joe called me into the living room and left me alone with Helen, who was very polite. She was a nice woman, in fact, and she listened sympathetically as I related the few details I could bring myself to tell her. She must have known I didn't want to talk to her. It would have been awkward enough talking to Sarah or any other close friend about my relationship with Anthony – had I wanted to talk about it at all. So I certainly wouldn't have chosen to talk to a stranger, however pleasant she was. But then, nothing was my choice any more.

'I'm not here to judge you,' Helen had said. 'I don't know if Joe told you, but I cheated on my husband a few years ago. I know Joe wants to know what happened between you and … Anthony – was that his name? But I just want to help you both.'

So I told her some basic details about what had happened and she made sympathetic noises. Then she went home and I never saw her again. I don't know if Joe did.

What I don't understand is why Helen agreed to get involved at all. I think Joe was hoping I might confide in her and tell her some detail I hadn't ever told him. Or perhaps he just saw it as another opportunity to humiliate me, by making me talk to a total stranger about something he knew I would never have chosen to discuss with anyone. But why had Helen gone along with it? It's a question, like so many others about my relationship with Joe, that I don't suppose will ever be answered.

Another extraordinary thing that Joe had started doing – much sooner after the discovery than I originally realised – was contacting all my old boyfriends. At first I thought he was lying when he said he'd spoken on the phone to Jack, the man I went out with for several years and who I thought at the time I was going to marry. But some of the things he knew made me think that it was probably true. What was even more shocking than his quizzing of Jack was that he'd also phoned Anthony.

I was mortified when Joe told me what he'd done, and very surprised, initially, that either of them had spoken to him at all. But, as I've said before, Joe can be very charming and persuasive, and usually gets what he wants eventually. And what he wanted on that occasion was to corroborate some of the things I'd told him, including some very intimate details of my past relationships – with people I'd been out with long before I ever met Anthony, let alone Joe himself.

I hadn't spoken to Jack at all since we'd broken up, and it was mortifying to hear Joe telling him, while I listened on speakerphone, that I was suffering from depression, had become so ill I was going to be sectioned, and that he was trying to help me. 'Did you know she'd had an affair with a married man after you broke up?' he asked Jack. 'Was she faithful to you while you were together?'

I was upset when Jack answered his questions and didn't just tell him to go to hell. He did ask, 'What's going on, Alice? Are you all right?' But I suppose he had no reason not to believe Joe's claim that he was trying to help me, particularly when I could hear what was being said and didn't contradict it myself. Perhaps he felt guilty too, and thought he was partly responsible for whatever was wrong with me, because he'd broken things off between us. Even so, to have answered questions like that, put to him by someone he didn't know – even someone as plausible and convincing as Joe – was an odd thing to do, and I did resent it a bit, for a while.

Joe also phoned a guy called Peter, who I'd been on three dates with eight years earlier. 'Why did you go out with him at all?' Joe had asked me one day. 'It was obvious from the emails he sent you that he was sleazy and only after one thing. And you expect me to believe that you didn't sleep with him? Oh come on, Alice. Really?'

'This is ridiculous,' I'd snapped. 'I don't need to defend my behaviour with Peter. I was single. I was twenty-two, for God's sake. I'd have no reason to be ashamed about it if I *had* slept with him. But I didn't.'

'I know,' Joe said at last. 'That's what *he* said, although it's always possible that you told him to deny it.'

I was horrified at the thought that Joe had rung a man I hadn't seen in years, and who I would now dread seeing again if our paths ever crossed professionally – assuming I did, one day, go back to work. 'How did you get his number? When did you speak to him? For God's sake,

Joe, are you going to check on every single relationship I've ever had, even the ones that weren't really relationships at all? Are you doing this to find out if I'm telling you the truth about my past boyfriends, or if I ever cheated on any of them? Or do you suspect that Anthony isn't the only married man I've had an affair with? Is that it, Joe? Despite everything I've told you, every tiny, embarrassing detail I've shared with you because you wanted to know, do you believe that I don't actually have the capacity to be faithful? I've told you – I don't know how many times – I didn't ever sleep with Anthony after I met you, and I didn't ever sleep with a married man before I met Anthony.'

'It's easy to get people's phone numbers,' Joe replied, answering the first question I'd asked him and ignoring everything else I'd said. 'I told him you'd tried to commit suicide and that, to be able to help you, I needed to know about the dates you'd had with him.'

'And he believed you?'

'Of course he believed me!' Joe sounded genuinely bemused by the question. 'Why wouldn't he? I'm very believable. You know that, Alice. And in answer to your other question: yes, I *am* going to contact all your past boyfriends. It's what happens when you realise that the person you're dealing with is an amoral whore. When you catch someone out in one lie, you can't believe anything they've ever told you. So you need to check it all.'

My friend Sarah was having none of it, though. 'I am not getting involved in this,' she told Joe when he phoned her. 'It's ridiculous.' Which made him more determined than ever that I wasn't to have any contact with her at all.

He used a different approach with Anthony, threatening to tell his wife if he didn't co-operate and answer the questions Joe asked him about our affair. I was appalled when I found out he'd spoken to him, and even more upset when he made me listen to one of his calls on speakerphone. He told me later that he'd written to Anthony's wife. And although I have no way of knowing if that's true, I felt sorry for Anthony – until I discovered that I was just one of many young women he'd had affairs with. Maybe, if Joe really did write to her, Anthony's wife learned something about her husband she needed to know.

When I found out about all the other women who'd lured Anthony away from his family, temporarily at least, I did wonder whether the story about his teenage daughter finding my message on his phone was a lie too – perhaps it was the excuse he used whenever he felt that the time had come to move on. Maybe his reaction when I told him I'd found someone else was more of a control thing, rather than genuine hurt and distress.

How did I get myself into these messes, I wondered. First compromising my own morality by getting involved with a married man who turned out to be the archetypal unfaithful husband whose wife doesn't understand him but who has 'never done this sort of thing before'. And then committing myself to the impossible, self-destructive task of trying to fix Joe.

Sometimes I stayed up for hours after Joe had gone to bed, writing the accounts he continued to insist on. One night, despite having drunk numerous cups of coffee to keep myself awake, I sat at the table in the living room, watching the sky turn from red to gold as the sun began to rise, and then crawled on to the sofa and fell asleep. And that's where Joe found me when he woke up, and he went ballistic because I hadn't finished what I was supposed to be writing.

One night, having drunk enough cups of coffee to be able to resist the temptation to close my eyes for a few minutes and get some rest, I stopped writing for a moment and read the words that were already scrawled across the page among many crossings-out.

'I am so, so sorry for everything that has happened,' I read. 'For the three stages of betrayal: the cheating; maintaining contact with Anthony behind your back; and lying about what really happened. Here is the final, true account of those events. When you have read it, please, please, please forgive me. All I want is to be with you. I *am* trustworthy and I would do anything for you. The lying and cheating are not me. Please believe me.'

On this occasion there were lists of questions Joe wanted me to answer about my relationship with Anthony.

How many nights had I spent with him? On this particular night, in this particular hotel, were there tissues on the table beside the bed? Had I had orgasms with him? What was I wearing on this occasion or that one? And there were other questions too, about other people.

As the sky grew lighter, I began to panic, knowing that as soon as Joe woke up he'd want to read the results of my night's labours. The problem was, it didn't matter how carefully I wrote each account or how many times I read it through to check it, there would always be something I'd missed, some tiny detail – insignificant to anyone except Joe – that was wrong, in that it didn't quite tally with a previous version, and that he would focus in on immediately, with all the deadly accuracy of a Stealth Bomber.

Forcing myself to calm down, I re-read the last paragraph one more time.

'I love you for your character, your integrity, your honesty. I love you for being the most genuine person I know. I love you for helping everyone you can – for going out of your way to help friends and family. You are the most handsome man I have ever met. I love you for helping me to see my potential and for giving me the courage to change my career to one that I feel passionate about and that is worthwhile. I know that with you I will be happy. I worry that without you I will never be truly happy, I will never get better and I will remain lost. With you at my side, I know that anything is achievable. I have never felt such an affinity with anyone. We are identically matched physically and emotionally. I know that I could spend a lifetime searching and no one would come close to you. I adore you and I'm desperate not to lose you. You are the love of my life. I am terrified that I've lost you because of what I've done and the lying. I'm begging you to take a leap of faith and believe in me and trust me. I know that it is a huge ask, considering what has happened and how I have acted, but I will not let you down. I am not the risk you think I am. I know that I can make you unbelievably happy. I know that we can have an amazing life together. Yours always, Alice.'

It wasn't a great piece of literature, I know, but it was the last paragraph of a very long account I'd been writing for hours, and I was exhausted. What was ironic about it was that, although I said how sorry I was for lying and how I would never lie to him again, there were parts of the account I wrote that night that would have been very different if I *had* only told the truth.

One of the most bizarre of the many bizarre experiences I had with Joe was taking a polygraph test. I'd answered and re-answered his questions for hour after hour, day after day, week after week. I'd written and re-written accounts and letters and lists of things I was going to do and buy for him. And he'd cross-examined my past boyfriends and, it seemed, any other man I'd ever had a drink or eaten a meal with. But he still didn't believe I was telling the truth about some of the things he wanted to know, some of which really did seem to matter to him, and some of which couldn't possibly have been important to anyone in their right mind. So I suppose, eventually, a lie-detector test was the inevitable next step.

In fact, I was the one who put the idea into his head, although it was a rhetorical question born of frustration when I said, 'Well, what do you want me to do – take a lie-detector test to prove I'm telling you the truth?' It was a stupid thing to say in the circumstances, and I shouldn't have been as taken aback as I was when Joe answered 'Yes'.

I didn't even know it was possible for people to have 'private' polygraph tests. But after phoning some of the companies that came up on a Google search, I discovered that, for a few hundred pounds, someone will come to your house to do one. It turns out that it's a service – like carpet cleaning or pest control, for example – and, although some of the companies offering it might not be wholly reputable, the one I found certainly was.

'It's our bread and butter,' the man I spoke to on the phone told me, 'one partner in a couple accusing the other of cheating.' Which is very sad when you think about it. What may be less common, however, is the potential 'liar' paying for the test herself, as I did. But I had long ago passed the point of no return in my commitment to trying to make Joe better and I had so much invested in his recovery that, like a lost-cause gambler, I kept thinking, 'Maybe this time.'

The man who came to the house one early evening, not long after Joe had got back from work, was called Dave. I don't know what I'd expected him to be like, but I was surprised by how 'normal' and nice he was, talking about his family and about his son who was eleven and just about to start secondary school.

I'd had to submit a list of questions in advance, all of which Joe had written and almost all of which were related to sex – had I had orgasms with the married man, for example, or had we ever had sex outside? Joe was so convinced the test would prove that I'd been lying, he'd worked himself up into quite a state of choking and dry retching. He held it together when our visitor arrived, though, as he always did when there was anyone else there, but when Dave went to the bathroom Joe hissed at me, 'Get this done as quickly as possible and get him out of here.'

When Dave came back from the bathroom, he told Joe he'd have to wait in another room while I did the test. For a moment, I thought he was going to refuse. But he must have realised, as I did, that it was a condition, not an option, and that agreeing to it was the only way he was going to get the answers he wanted. So although he was very rude to Dave, he did go upstairs, where we could hear him pacing the floor above our heads, like a caged animal.

I don't know why, but I was surprised to find that a 'real' polygraph test is done using the same equipment and techniques as you see in films. I sat on a wooden dining chair with a couple of coiled straps stretched across my chest and things that looked like tiny blood-pressure cuffs around two of my fingers, with wires that linked them to a laptop on the table behind me, where I couldn't see it.

I could tell Dave was doing his best to make everything seem normal and mundane, but I was already stressed before the test began, and anxious in case my nervousness affected the results and made it look as though I was lying when I wasn't. As he was strapping me to the machine, I'd asked Dave how reliable the results really were, and his answer had been '99-point-something'. But he would say that, wouldn't he? And as I sat there, with the soles of my bare feet making damp patches on the wooden floor, I had to keep telling myself, 'It'll be okay. You've got nothing to hide.'

Dave must have realised that I was working myself up into a state of panic – or maybe he was just used to people in my position being overly anxious – and he tried to put my mind at rest by saying, 'Don't worry. It's natural to be apprehensive. That's why we always start with some base-line questions, so that we can establish some parameters that will enable us to interpret the results specifically in relation to you.' The problem was, there were some things I *had* lied to Joe about.

About four months after the discovery, I'd decided that if Joe refused to believe me when I told him the truth about my sexual relationship with Anthony, I'd lie about it. It was stupid, but I thought it might shut him up if I told him I'd had orgasms with Anthony that had been almost as good as the ones I had with him. It didn't, of course, because then he wanted to know how many times, when, where … After that, I sometimes alternated between telling the truth and lying, trying to second-guess the answers he wanted to hear on a particular day, but almost always failing, so that every answer to every question became punctuated by violence.

The night before the polygraph test he'd asked me again, and again hadn't believed me when I told him the truth – that I hadn't enjoyed sex with Anthony and hadn't ever had an orgasm with him. 'What does it matter anyway?' I wanted to shout at him. 'How could it possibly help you to know about the sex I had with another man before I even knew you?' But, for some reason, it did matter to Joe. So much so, in fact, that he was obsessed by it. Well, in a few minutes he'd have definitive answers to his questions. Then maybe he'd finally stop asking them.

The first question Dave asked me was whether I was taking the test under any duress. If I hadn't had to give only yes/no answers, I could have said, 'Everything I do is under duress.' Instead, I lied and answered 'No'.

'Is your name Alice Keale?'

It was probably the simplest question I was going to be asked, but already my hands were sweating and I could hear the pulse of my heart beat in my head as I said 'Yes'.

'Are you thirty-two years old?'

'Yes.' Surely the light from the lamp on the table in front of me wasn't usually that bright. 'Breathe,' I told myself. 'In. Out. In …'

He asked a few other mundane questions, and then, in exactly the same tone of voice, said, 'Did you orgasm with Anthony?'

'No,' I answered, almost without thinking. And then, to myself, 'Please let it show that I'm telling the truth. Please let something go my way, just this once.'

Joe was still pacing backwards and forwards in the room above us, the sound of his footsteps like a deliberate reminder that he was there. Why couldn't he just sit down for a few minutes and let me do this in peace, I wondered. Was he trying to put me off, to make me so nervous I failed the test? If that *was* what he was trying to do, he was coming close to succeeding. Dave must have realised that too, because he excused himself for a moment and left the room, after which I could hear muffled voices, his low and even, Joe's louder and abrupt. He did stop pacing after that, though, which made it a bit easier for me to focus on the questions I was being asked.

Dave asked them all in the same neutral tone.

'Do you like chocolate?'

'Yes.'

'Did you and Anthony have sex outside?'

'No.'

Then eventually, after what seemed like an eternity of answering questions, he said, 'Okay, we're done.'

'And …?' My voice was barely a whisper.

'You've passed. One hundred per cent. You told the truth on every count.'

'I'll get Joe,' I said. But when Dave unstrapped the monitors and I tried to stand up, it felt as though every muscle in my body had turned to water and for a moment I thought I was going to fall.

When I came back into the room with Joe a few seconds later, Dave told him the results. 'I'll print them out when I get back to the office,' he said, 'and send them to you in the post.' I glanced at Joe while Dave was speaking and felt a sudden rush of love and sympathy for him, in part because the unguarded expression of relief I saw on his face made me him look like a vulnerable little boy.

He was right, I thought: it *had* all been my fault. In those first few idyllic weeks we were together, he'd believed that he could trust me. And then he discovered that I'd been sending emails to another man. But it was

235

the things I'd written to Anthony in those emails that were the real lies – telling him I missed him and that it wasn't really over between us. I'd said them because I was a coward, and then I'd compounded my dishonesty by lying about them to Joe too, because I was afraid of losing him. Now, after all the violence and misery of the last few months, he finally knew I'd been telling him the truth.

It was less than half an hour after Dave had left the house when Joe's questions started again. Another half an hour later, he was shouting in my face as he banged my head repeatedly against the bedroom wall. By the time I went to bed, in the early hours of the morning, there were fresh bite marks on my arms and breasts. And, again, I blamed myself, for being so stupid as to believe that the lie-detector test had been anything other than a ridiculous charade and for not realising that there *was* no 'truth' that could ever make Joe better.

Chapter 15

I met most of Joe's family during the first few months we were together. His mother was the only one I met before the discovery, when we had lunch with her in a restaurant on the way back from Devon to London after spending the weekend with my parents. And then she came to stay with us for a couple of days after Christmas.

'She mustn't know about your affair with a married man,' Joe had told me. 'If she knew, she'd make me leave you.' I could never really be certain that he was telling the truth, either entirely or in part, and I didn't know if he was on that occasion, or if the reason he wanted to hide my 'sordid affair' from his mother was that he thought it would remind her of what had been an incredibly distressing time in her life – as it had been in Joe's young life too, from what he'd told me – when her own husband left her for another woman. In fact, though, his warning wasn't necessary, as it wasn't something I'd ever willingly have told anyone. It was Joe who insisted on revealing it to my family and friends and to anyone else we ever had any contact with.

I didn't tell Joe's mother about the way he was behaving either. It isn't a conversation I could imagine having with anyone's parents, although after I'd met his father I did wonder if I should have said something to him. I had hoped that his mother's presence would give me a break from the questioning and violence, and maybe calm him down long enough for him to realise that punishing me wasn't going to make either of us happy again.

In the event, of course, the visit by Joe's mother didn't change anything. His physical and verbal attacks contin-ued throughout the entire time she was with us, but quietly, in the bedroom, and on the many 'emergency errands' he found we had to run during her stay. She must have thought we were quite mad, darting in and out of the living room every few minutes and suddenly remember-ing something we had to pop out and buy at the local shops. In fact, Joe told me afterwards that she'd said she thought *I* was very odd because of it.

What was really hard to believe was that Joe's mother didn't *hear* anything, even when we were in the bedroom and Joe had his hands around my neck, squeezing the breath out of me. I prayed while she was staying with us that she'd pick up on the fact – which seemed blatantly obvious to me – that there was something wrong, because then she'd have to help us. I desperately wanted to tell her what her son was doing to me. I even imagined waking her up in the middle of the night when Joe had finally gone to sleep, showing her the marks his hands had made around my neck and begging her to help me. Or that Joe would lose it in front of her and start hitting me, so that she'd be forced to do something.

Even if she hated me when she found out how badly I'd hurt her son emotionally, surely not even the most doting mother would fail to intervene if she knew her child was violently abusing someone. At the very least, she'd want to stop him running the risk of ruining the rest of his life by ending up in prison because he'd injured me, or worse. But although Joe often appeared to lose control when he was attacking me, he always seemed to be able to maintain it when he needed to – in front of his mother, for example.

It was largely that ability to switch from vicious to charming in the blink of an eye that made me begin to wonder how much of what Joe did was due to mental illness and how much was simply cold calculation. I suppose a simplistic explanation for his behaviour would be that his childhood had been miserable because his father had left his mother for another woman, which had thrown his mother into the depths of despair, deprived Joe of a resident father and made him feel that he wasn't as 'good' as the other boys at school. So now he was punishing me, as the epitome of the woman who stole his dad – and who, as things turned out, subsequently lost him to another woman, who lost him to another …

Although no one had any idea about the extent of Joe's abuse, everyone who knew anything about it, including my psychiatrist, told me that his behaviour wasn't normal. But although I wanted to believe that he was having a mental breakdown, because that would mean he wasn't responsible for what was happening, it began to seem increasingly likely that he always knew exactly what he was doing. However frenzied and out of control he appeared to be, he always stopped within a hair's breadth of going too far, and he always treated me quite differently in front of other people, although we rarely saw anyone else, because my family and friends had been judged to be 'inappropriate', and Joe didn't seem to have any friends at all.

A few weeks after the discovery, we went to stay with Joe's dad for a weekend. He seemed like a nice man, and obviously loved his son. But Joe made me tell him about my affair with Anthony, and no visit was going to be anything but hugely uncomfortable after a conversation like that.

I didn't realise it at the time, but I'm sure the whole situation was planned and contrived by Joe. Just as he had reasons for *not* wanting his mother to know about my affair, I could see how, in his twisted, vindictive mind, he felt that his father *should* know, although I think he suspected, even before I told him, that *something* was going on.

It was actually his dad talking about an exhibition he'd seen at a gallery Joe knew I'd worked in with Anthony that triggered the process leading to the revelation. We'd gone for a walk in the countryside – Joe and I, his dad and his dad's current wife – and when his dad mentioned the name of the gallery Joe gagged, then turned his back on us and walked away. He was only gone for a couple of minutes, but although he said he was fine when he came back it must have been clear to both of them that something was wrong.

The problem was, Joe had a lot of triggers, which had increased exponentially the more details he made me tell him about my affair with Anthony. It could be as simple as someone mentioning a town where he knew we'd stayed together; or hearing a forecast for rain on a weather report after I'd mentioned – in response to close questioning – that it had been raining on one of the nights we'd spent together; or just seeing a woman wearing a skirt or top in a particular colour. And it meant that every television programme and every interaction we ever had with anyone was incredibly tense, because I always knew that we were just one, apparently innocent, word away from Joe going into a decline.

He got upset again that night and left the room while we were having dinner with his father and stepmother. I would have given anything to have been able to stay there, talking, as we had been doing until then, about the sort of normal, everyday things most people talk about around the dinner table. But I excused myself and followed Joe into the bedroom.

'I need you to tell my dad what you've done,' he said, when I asked him if he was all right. And although I did argue with him for a while, it was only half-heartedly, because I knew he'd win in the end, and that all I was doing was delaying what was, after all, just another in a whole catalogue of humiliating experiences.

By the time I came out of the bedroom, Joe's step-mother was clearing the dining table and his dad was in the living room, which is where I went to talk to him. I can't remember exactly how I phrased it, something along the lines of 'Joe wants me to tell you something. I don't know how to say it. It's something I'm very ashamed of …'

I was too mortified on my own behalf to wonder how my confession would strike someone in Joe's dad's situation – a man who, some thirty years earlier, had had an affair with a woman that led to the break-up of his marriage and to what was, in effect, the abandonment of his young son. He was very nice about it, though, basically just saying, 'Thank you for telling me.' I suppose what he might have asked was, '*Why* are you telling me?' But perhaps he already knew, because he did say, 'You can stay here for a bit if you'd like to.' And although *he* wasn't a touchy-feely type of person, his wife came into the bedroom later, when I was there on my own, and gave me a hug. In fact, they both seemed to be lovely people.

It seems impossible now to think that we struggled for more than a year. I suppose you can get used to anything after a while, particularly if you don't think there's any alternative. That's something else I still don't understand, the fact that, for all those months, I thought I had no choice when, in reality, there's always a choice, as long you're free physically to come and go, as I was. The problem for many people in many situations, however, is that a mental prison can be considerably more difficult to break out of than a physical one. It's surprising how quickly and easily someone can become isolated and dependent on someone else, emotionally, financially and in every other way, so that they lose the ability to think for themselves or to be certain about what's reasonable, and what isn't. I know I would have found it difficult to believe that it could happen to someone like me, before I met Joe.

One day, almost a year after I'd moved in with Joe, he told me he couldn't bear to have me around any more. He had started drinking quite a bit by that time and was taking sleeping tablets too, to try to knock himself out at night, although they didn't really work. It seemed that everything I said or did reminded him of the terrible thing I'd done all those months ago, to the point that just the sight of me made him ill, he said.

I'd forgotten many of the details he'd made me go over and over during the months since we'd become locked together in what I was only just beginning to realise was a mutually destructive relationship. Joe remembered them all, however, and he talked incessantly about the past, like someone possessed. Sometimes, he'd suddenly stop what he was doing, bend almost double and start to dry retch, and sometimes he couldn't get out of bed at all for entire days. Then, one day, he told me, 'The company's going to let me go in two months. I had a meeting with someone from HR earlier this week. I'm not getting the job done because of you, Alice. Because of what you did to me. And now I'm going to lose it.' I don't know if any part of what he was said was true. Maybe someone from HR did have a word with him. But he certainly didn't lose his job.

Whatever the real reason was, Joe sent me home to my parents, while he – apparently – spent the next few days alone in his house in London, in bed. I thought he'd do what he normally did and tell me to get off the train before I got there and go back. But he didn't, and I stayed at my parents' house for the next four months, returning to visit Joe for just occasional days. Then, one day, he phoned me and said, 'It's not working. My therapist says it's not working. I think we have to accept that it's never going to work. We're too toxic for each other, Alice.'

At first, I didn't understand what he meant. Even when it dawned on me that what he was telling me was that our relationship was over, I couldn't make any sense of what he was saying. Because Joe had promised me, sworn to me, that he'd never leave me, no matter what.

'But I don't want it to end,' I told him. 'I won't leave you, Joe. I love you.' Anyone who knew about the nightmare I'd been living for all those months would have thought that what I was saying sounded crazy. To me, though, it was perfectly logical, because there was a reason why I'd put up with the horrific violence and mental abuse, which was that, one day, I'd have paid the price for what I'd done and Joe would be all right again. That was the whole point of everything: to fix Joe. It was the end I'd kept in sight throughout all the miserable months when there had been no other apparent reason for my existence. I didn't work, I didn't see my family or friends, I didn't have any money, or self-esteem. But none of that would matter when I had the real Joe back again.

I wasn't certain about many things any more. What I was certain about, however, was that everything I'd tolerated and sacrificed could not have been for nothing.

As I listened to Joe's voice on the phone, I was sitting on my bed in my parents' house, staring at the shelves on the yellow-painted walls that held all the books I used to read and the CDs I used to play when I was a teenager, with one arm clutching my knees to my chest like a shield and hot tears rolling down my cheeks, thinking, 'This can't be real. This can't be my life, to be thirty-three years old and have nothing.'

'We can't be in contact now,' Joe said. 'I doubt that we ever can be again. We just don't work together, Alice. You know that I love you, don't you? You know that you're the love of my life?' Then the line went dead and he'd gone.

Falling back on to the bed, I pulled the duvet over my head and closed my eyes. He didn't mean it, I told myself. It was just another of his tests, another way of making me pay for what I'd done. Yes, that was it. Of course he hadn't suddenly decided after all these months, after everything I'd done to try to make amends, that things weren't going to work out after all.

I dialled his number, then listened to it ring and ring, before eventually going to voicemail. Even then, I didn't hear his voice, because he'd changed it to an automated message. How could he say what he'd just said to me and then not answer? How dare he? *I* always had to answer when he phoned, whatever time of the day or night it was. For me, there were no excuses. If Joe rang – as he did several times every day – I answered the phone. That was the way it had been for months. So how could this be fair? Hadn't we written a list of rules, which I had adhered to religiously? Our rules, we'd called them, although they were Joe's. Well, answering the phone when the other person rang was one of those rules, and it was only fair that it applied to him just as much as it did to me.

I pushed the duvet off my head and examined the crappy little phone he'd made me buy, to replace my iPhone, which he said triggered painful thoughts for him about my past. 'If you ever buy another iPhone,' he'd said, 'it will be over between us. I won't even be able to remain your friend. But why would you want one anyway? Surely it would only make you feel sick to have such a reminder of your amoral past? Whereas this phone, simple and straightforward, will be a reminder to you of how you've changed, and of how you're now a reformed woman with an intact, fully functioning moral code.'

Well, I'd stuck to my side of the bargain – for months. I'd answered his phone calls. I'd followed the rules. And now he was saying it was all over anyway.

In retrospect, it was ridiculous to have reacted the way I did, not least because the reality was that I hated my life. I'd hated it every single day since the discovery. There had been countless occasions when I'd wished I had the strength to walk away from Joe, or, failing that, that someone would help me. The irony was that, now Joe had given me the freedom I'd longed for, I didn't want it. Because although he'd actually been destroying me, it felt to me as though he'd been propping me up. And when he suddenly stepped away, he let me fall.

What *was* true, however, was that he was the only thing I had left, and I couldn't bear to face the prospect of having nothing at all.

That night when Joe rang me, and I listened to him telling me that it was over, the moonlight was streaming into my bedroom through the curtains I hadn't bothered to close. I love the night sky, especially in the countryside where my parents live, where the light from the stars isn't all but obliterated by street lights. But the moon that night seemed to be like a spotlight, shining into the bedroom and illuminating all the things I'd kept from my childhood, as if to say, 'You built a good life for yourself when you left home. Now you're back where you started more than fifteen years ago.'

I tried to contact Joe countless times over the next few weeks. Sometimes I sat in my room staring at my phone for hours on end, willing it to ring. But he didn't ever answer my calls or texts, except for one, about a week after he told me it was over. After phoning and texting him many times without a response, I decided not to try to contact him at all, just to see what he'd do, and he phoned me that evening. But he didn't really say anything; he just asked me how I was, and then hung up when I asked him, 'How could you do this to me, Joe?' I suppose that once he knew he'd regained control there wasn't anything else he needed to say.

That was more than two years ago now, and although I continued to call him intermittently for the next six months, it was the last time I ever spoke to him.

I had what people call a nervous breakdown after Joe sent me home. I lived at my parents' house – causing them a huge amount of worry, I know – and couldn't get out of bed for weeks. It felt as though there wasn't a single part of my life that hadn't been adversely affected by my relationship with him. My mum made an appointment for me to see the GP I'd had before I'd left home and gone to live in London, who was very nice. But as I didn't have any money to pay for the therapy I needed, my name was dropped into the black hole of NHS mental health care.

The depression that had first surfaced when I was at university, but had then been kept more or less under control, got a lot worse during those first few months. I also started getting panic attacks and flashbacks to the most violent incidents that had occurred during the time I'd spent with Joe, and I would find myself gasping for breath and incapacitated by fear. I still get them sometimes now, although they're not as frequent or as severe as they used to be. It turned out that what I was experiencing were classic symptoms of post-traumatic stress disorder – PTSD – which is the diagnosis that was made by the psychiatrist I saw about three months after my name had been added to the waiting list.

So then I was put on a waiting list to have therapy with a clinical psychologist. I'm still waiting, more than eighteen months later. I did eventually get six sessions with a counsellor. The trouble is that, for most people, six sessions isn't enough. And although the counsellor I had was lovely, she wasn't trained specifically to deal with victims of domestic abuse – which is how I'd be classified. So instead of achieving the magic cure I think I was hoping for, I ended up being left with all sorts of highlighted but unresolved issues, which just made me feel worse.

One of the many things I hated about the way I felt at that time – and still feel to some extent now – was the sense of being helpless. When I was working, before I met Joe, I used to pay to see a psychiatrist every few months, and for a CBT session whenever I felt I needed one, which made me feel as though I was in control of my mental health, rather than my mental health being in control of me. But by the time I really needed help I'd spent all my money on holidays and gifts for Joe, and could no longer afford to take care of myself. And that made me angry, which only added to my distress.

My parents tried to help me, but they couldn't afford to pay for the kind of care I really needed. And my GP tried too, although there wasn't really anything she could do unless I was suicidal, in which case I would be admitted to a psychiatric ward; but she really didn't want that to happen, she told me, because she thought it would do me far more harm than good. We looked into going down the charity route too, but their waiting lists are even longer.

It's an indescribably horrible feeling, desperately wanting help and finding that there's none available to you.

Chapter 16

I had a couple of appointments booked with the psychiatrist, but she was away at the time of the second one and I saw a locum, who increased the dosage of my antidepressants. But that just made me feel numb, not better, and didn't actually *deal* with anything.

Things did start to improve a bit with time, and after a few weeks I was at least able to get out of bed and do some basic things. Everyone kept telling me that 'time heals'. I just didn't realise it takes so long. Even a year after Joe's last phone call, the agony would still be there. Maybe the volume had been turned down slightly, but it was still playing on a continuous loop in the background, like a constant, cacophonous soundtrack to my life.

For the time being, every day was painful, and far too long. How could fifteen hours, or however long I'd been awake, seem so interminable? The best part of each day – if anything so unremittingly miserable can be said to have a 'best part' – was just after I woke up, those few seconds when my mind was blank and I wasn't aware of what I'd lost, or what I'd become. It's true that ignorance is bliss; it certainly was for me in those blissfully ignorant first-waking moments of every day, before reality hit me like a physical blow, and the agony returned.

I did try to make the pain go away, but not during those first few weeks, when any sort of trying seemed to be out of the question, and when I could lie completely still in my bed for hours, just staring at the same patch of wall without really seeing it. I'd think I was thinking, but my mind was actually completely blank, and hours would seem like minutes. Sometimes I'd imagine myself getting out of bed, going into the bathroom and having a shower, making a cup of coffee and then going for a walk, or even just wanting to eat something. Then depression and apathy would take over again, and even just imagining doing those things was exhausting.

Although I often used to wish I didn't have to struggle any more, I didn't ever consider taking my own life – for reasons that I think were actually more positive than simply not having the physical or mental energy to do it. What was really driving me crazy was wanting to know *why* Joe did what he did to me.

'It wasn't your fault,' my family and friends told me patiently. 'He's not well. You're not responsible for the emotional and physical abuse he subjected you to.' And I tried to believe them. But after all those months of Joe telling me it *was* my fault – added to the guilt I already felt for having had an affair with a married man – there's a part of my brain that still thinks he's right. What was certainly true, however, was that only Joe could answer the question I *needed* to have an answer to: 'Why?'

What I also wanted to know – and still do – is if he really did believe that, by doing any of the multitude of things he told me to do during the months when we were so unhappy together, I really would be able to fix him. Or was he just playing a malevolent game with me, enjoying his role as puppeteer? It's frustrating and disconcerting not to have answers to any of the questions I still ask myself on a fairly regular basis. Perhaps it's time to accept the fact that I never will.

I *want* to move on and leave the past where it belongs. But I also want Joe to have to account for what he did. I'd like him to have to listen while some medically qualified person, whose opinion he can't dismiss, tells him that his reaction was out of all proportion to what I'd done and that there was no excuse for the way he treated me.

I hate the fact that I kept trying to contact him after he told me it was over. Apart from there being no rational explanation for my wanting to have anything to do with a man who had been abusing me for more than a year, it put him firmly back in the driving seat – in control to the bitter end. For a long time, I wanted him to be the weak one for a change and to phone me – even send me a text – to say he realised he had been in the wrong and that he was sorry. In the end, it took six months before I'd built up just enough self-esteem to stop calling *him*.

Something else I deeply regret is that I didn't have the guts to be the one who ended it. I wish, too, that I hadn't spent all my money; that I wasn't facing the prospect of starting my adult life all over again; that I was able to work in the world I was working in when I met Joe, but which I know he'll use his considerable influence to ensure is closed to me now; that I didn't have nightmares; and that I could have the old me back again.

But despite wishing all those things could be different, I know I'm lucky in many ways, not least because I don't feel trapped by Joe's abuse any more. Not that I feel free – the PTSD still keeps me locked inside the memories. I'm lucky, too, to have good friends and a loving family, who are doing everything they can to make sure I succeed in creating a new life for myself. I know there's no magic bullet and that it's going to take time for the damage to be repaired and the psychological wounds to heal, but I *will* rebuild my life. It'll be different from the life I imagined I'd have when I left university. But that's true for lots of people, for lots of reasons. All I need now is to find some reason to be happy.

Although my family and friends have been incredibly supportive, when something bad has happened in your life there comes a point when people expect you to snap out of it, pull yourself together, pick yourself up and get back on track. Even though they might not say anything, you know it's what they must be thinking. And it's a reasonable expectation from their point of view. The problem is, I still sometimes doubt whether I will ever be able to return to my old self.

One day, after I'd stopped spending every day in bed but was still living at my parents' house, I wandered into the garage and started looking through some of the boxes of my belongings that had been stored there, waiting to be moved to … who knows where? Among them, I found a plain brown shoebox into which I'd put everything I'd kept from my relationship with Joe. There was a book about Peru, about the Inca trail we'd trekked, which I'd bought for him, but which, for some reason, I'd ended up with myself. There were ticket stubs from films, plays and operas we'd seen together, of whose plots I had no recollection at all, because even in a theatre Joe's questions and accusations used to continue, until eventually someone would tell him, angrily, to be quiet. There were plane tickets too, from our first, wonderful trip together to Barcelona, and from all the other expensive and desperately miserable holidays I'd paid for, to magical destinations that will now be linked forever in my mind with violence and fear.

There was just one photograph in the shoebox, of me and Joe standing on a mountain on the Inca trail under a cloudless sky, smiling and with our arms linked. Anyone looking at that photograph would be struck by how happy I am, unless they knew me well and looked more closely, when they would see the anxiety in my eyes and the stiffness of my stance.

The shoebox had arrived at my parents' house in a van one day, sent by Joe with all the other belongings I'd left at his house when he sent me away. It was hard to believe it contained the only evidence I had left of fifteen months of indescribable pain.

'Surely you'll want to throw it all away,' my sister said when I told her about it. And that certainly would have been the healthy thing to do. But, for some reason I still don't understand, I *needed* to keep it. Maybe it felt as though it was the only proof I had that those months with Joe were real and that I hadn't imagined it all, or dreamed about it in some horrific nightmare. One day I *will* be strong enough to dump that shoebox in a bin, or burn it on the fire. But not yet.

Seven months after Joe sent me away, I emailed to my sister and best friend the account I'd written shortly after I first went home. I hadn't talked to anyone except my psychiatrist about what Joe had done to me, and when I pressed 'Send' on the laptop it felt in a way like the final betrayal of his trust. Then I was angry with myself for feeling guilty about revealing just some of the details of his abuse to people who really do love me. After I'd sent it, though, the anger and guilt were outweighed by a huge sense of relief, as though someone had, quite literally, lifted out of my hands the massive weight I'd been carrying around with me for almost two years. What I didn't realise until some time later was that, by sharing some of my experiences that day, I had taken a significant step on the road to my recovery.

I had a colleague at work, before I met Joe, who told me one day that she often fantasised about winning the lottery. 'I know everyone does it,' she said. 'But I got to the point where I'd taken it to what I think is probably an unhealthy level. I would imagine the car I'd buy, the house I'd purchase and how I'd decorate it. In fact, I not only picked out the wallpaper for every room, I ordered samples of each one. That's when I realised I'd gone too far and needed to stop. And the stupid thing is, I only buy a lottery ticket once in a blue moon.'

Some of what she told me was very funny, while some of it did sound a bit extreme. But at the other end of the spectrum is not fantasising at all, which is probably just as bad. So I was relieved when, for the first time 'after Joe', I found myself trying to imagine what my life might be like in the future. It was about a year since I'd last heard from him and I was sick of having no job, no social life, and nothing to think about except the past. So I imagined that I'd rebuilt my life and was happy. It was a disheartening exercise in some respects, but the positive thing that came out of it was realising that I would eventually be able to move on.

Something else I sometimes imagine is bumping into Joe on the street. In one scenario, he's become the man I thought he was when we first met and we get back together and work things out. In another, I'm very happy and successful, obviously not only surviving but thriving without him, and I just nod at him, then walk away without a second glance, leaving him deeply regretting having lost me.

The truth is, however, that Joe's career is going from strength to strength, while I'm in the process of starting all over again. And although I've come a long way in the last few months, from the time when I was spending every day in bed at my parents' house, crying and dialling Joe's number over and over again on my phone, I'm still not 'happy and successful' – certainly not to an extent that would elicit envy and regret in Joe. So I don't know how I'd react if I bumped into him, and I'm not sure that I want to find out.

I'm managing, though, mostly because I'm able, most of the time, to mask the real me – who's almost paralysed by depression – with the pretend me – who's content and doing well. My doctor tells me, gently, to try to find the middle ground, that being 'okay' is good enough, and that I don't have to pretend. I know he's right, but, somehow, I don't seem to cope so well on the middle ground, because if I allow even a tiny part of the pain to show, it ends up overwhelming me. And once I start to cry, I can't stop. So that's why I pretend. If I push all the negative thoughts to the back of my mind and concentrate only on what I'm doing now, I can stay calm – for a while, at least, until the slowly expanding ball of pain inside me prevents me from breathing, and I have to stop what I'm doing while I wait for it to shrink again.

Unfortunately, not being with Joe any more hasn't banished my sense of guilt. Not about having had an affair with a married man – it was wrong and I'm sorry I did it, but I'm not going to beat myself up about it for the rest of my life. But about the fact that, because I didn't report Joe's behaviour to the police, he might be doing to some other poor woman what he did to me.

I did phone the police one day and asked, 'If I wanted to make a statement about something but not take any further action, could you just file it away somewhere, so that it's on record if the person concerned ever does something similar in the future?' But they said they couldn't, and that if I reported a crime to them they would have to investigate it, which I'm still too scared to let them do.

Although my mum really wanted me to talk to the police, so that Joe would be made accountable for what he'd done to me, my sister could understand why I wouldn't do it. I wasn't just afraid for myself; I was frightened for my family, because Joe always told me that if I ever did go to the police he'd sue my family for defamation and make sure they were ruined financially. And I was also frightened for Joe's next potential victim, particularly after my therapist told me that it's probable, rather than merely possible, that he *will* do the same thing to someone else.

It was that last fear that prompted me to talk to a friend who's a lawyer – although not in the field of domestic abuse – who told me, 'I know it's terribly unfair, but I really don't think you'd be able to cope emotionally with taking legal action against him. And God forbid you lost the case. What then? I can't begin to imagine how that would make you feel. And losing *is* a real possibility, because of the lack of proof.'

'I know you're right,' I said. 'I'm just going to have to find some way of coming to terms with the fact that he's got away with what he did and will carry on living his life as if nothing had ever happened!'

In fact, psychological and emotional abuse has only very recently become a crime, with abusers facing up to five years in prison for 'coercive, controlling behaviour' towards their partners, spouses or family members. The abuse has to be reported within two years of it occurring. But although it would be possible for Joe to be prosecuted under the new law, I know it would be a case of my word against his, because I don't have any proof of what he did to me. The only record of it that exists are the reports that were made when my family were worried about me, which include my statement to the police officers who came to Joe's house, in which I denied being abused by him in any way.

The other barrier to any kind of legal action is that Joe is very believable. I can just imagine him explaining in court that, although he doesn't want to blame me – 'In view of the fact that she suffers from depression and has done some things which, quite frankly, Your Honour, are not the sort of things you'd expect a moral, sane person to do' – he is completely bemused by my accusations. And even if I did have irrefutable proof of his abuse – including the physical violence he subjected me to on a regular basis – I don't know if my mental health would withstand everything that would be involved in instigating a case against him.

So although I think I'll always feel a sense of resentment about the fact that Joe hasn't had to account for his actions, I realised after the conversation I had with my lawyer friend that it was time to move on. And that what's I'm trying to do now, although there are still days when normal life is bowling along surprisingly smoothly and then something happens or someone says something that makes me feel as though I've been punched in the stomach. For example, there's a really nice girl at work who told me the other day that she'd had an affair with a married man. 'I felt terrible about it,' she said. 'So obviously I didn't want to tell my parents. But I also didn't want to compound one underhand thing with another. And when I did tell them they were great. They weren't very pleased about it, as you can imagine, and they said all the things you'd expect them to say. But then they were just like, "So now learn from it and move on."'

It seemed so unfair that she'd made the same mistake I'd made and come through it relatively unscathed, while my mother still says she won't ever be able to forgive me. Now, though, when something upsets my still very tentative equilibrium – like the girl at work telling me about her parents' mild reaction to her relationship with a married man – I remind myself that what happened to me could have been much worse. I could have had Joe's child, for example, and then I would have been trapped forever.

I know that, eventually, a day *will* pass when I don't think about the months I spent with Joe, and that I've already made more progress than I ever thought would be possible. In fact, even just a few weeks ago I couldn't have told my story at all.

Chapter 17

I knew that the worst was over and that I was on the road to recovery – however long and rocky it might prove to be – when I started doing some of the things Joe had always forbidden me to do. There was a list – of course – which included the following, among many others.

- No watching the weather forecast, the news, certain television programmes and films – because, in Joe's mind, they had some tenuous link to the married man.
- No looking in the mirror, or even in the general direction of a mirror.
- No long hair – he took care of that one himself with a pair of nail scissors.
- No wearing of jeans, certain styles of dresses, shorts; no underwear in certain colours – basically, no wearing of any clothes like those I'd worn when I was seeing Anthony.

If You Love Me

- No shaving of legs or regular attention to any other kind of personal grooming.
- No make-up to be worn except on specific occasions, and with Joe's permission.
- Hair to be washed no more than every other day.
- No iPhone.
- No phone with any camera, video or internet connection.
- No digital camera.
- No keeping of old photographs or videos – all of which had to be destroyed, because everything and everyone who had been part of my life before I met Joe didn't matter any more.
- All contact with family and friends to be kept to a minimum, and to be strictly under Joe's supervision.
- No social life that hadn't been agreed by Joe, and none at all that didn't include him.
- No sleeping during the day.
- No going into the bedroom during the day.
- No deleting of internet browsing history – which would always be checked and monitored by Joe.
- No phone calls except those approved by Joe – all phone bills were itemised and he checked every detail.
- No going anywhere without first asking Joe's permission.
- No working – and no mention of the word 'career' in relation to myself.

- No use of certain other words, including any with the suffix 'wise' – as in 'work-wise'.
- No use of certain phrases such as 'to be honest'.
- No visits to … The list of places I wasn't allowed to visit was far too long to include here.

It was childish to start working my way through the list. But it made me feel like a real person again to watch television programmes Joe had expressly forbidden, to channel-hop so that I caught five weather forecasts in a row, to spend minutes at a time pulling faces at myself in the mirror, to wait until my parents had gone to work and then run around the house dressed in jeans and a black bra shouting, 'To be honest, I think that, work-wise, and to all intents and purposes …'

The rule about not wearing jeans had come into force just a few days after the discovery, when Joe asked me, 'Does wearing jeans remind you of him – because you were wearing them when you first got involved with him? Is that why you persist in wearing them? Do you have no morals at all, Alice?'

Then, one day, after I'd been living with my parents for a few months, my sister Lucy said, 'You used to wear jeans almost all the time. I think it's time for you to buy some more.' So we went shopping together, and as I stood in front of the mirror in the changing room I started to cry. I cried a lot at that time, and when I'd pulled myself together I bought two pairs that day. Then, as I tapped my new PIN number into the card reader at the till, I had a sudden moment of panic. 'Oh my God, he'll know,' I told Lucy, before remembering that he wouldn't, because he no longer had access to my bank account and couldn't examine every transaction and demand to know what I'd bought. So I could wear jeans every single day for the rest of my life if I wanted to.

I bought an iPhone too, as soon as I could afford one. The phone I'd had when I met Joe was a symbol of my amorality, according to him, and he'd made me smash it into a thousand pieces. So when a new iPhone went on sale a few months ago, I fantasised about buying one in every available colour and having a different one for every day of the week. I didn't, of course; I just bought one. But it was nice to think that I *could* have done so if I'd really wanted to.

Joe would never know I was doing all the things he hadn't allowed me to do, and he wouldn't have cared if he had known. To me, though, it was all part of getting my life back and of realising that it hadn't been completely destroyed, along with all my old videos and photographs. Having said that, I know I'm still a long way from being 'fixed', and there will probably always be things that trigger the sense of something very close to despair that sometimes overwhelms me.

One example was when Lucy got married recently, and I was a bridesmaid at her wedding. I love my sister very much. I don't know how I would have coped over the last couple of years without her support. So it was wonderful to see how happy she looked as she walked down the aisle towards her husband-to-be, Simon. But I felt something else too, something that made me very ashamed of myself, because it was very much like envy. My sister has a lovely home, a good career, a very bright future and was about to marry a man she loved and who loved her. And, in that moment, I longed to step into her shoes, to trade places with her so that all those good things – the things I thought I was going to have with Joe when I first met him – were in *my* grasp.

'Compare and despair' is what my therapist calls it. 'No good will come of it,' she told me. 'It will only make you feel miserable. So concentrate instead on your achievements, on all the positives in your own life.' But sometimes I can't see anything positive in my life. Sometimes I just want to stop having to try so hard to take even the smallest step forward, and give up. Those moments of despair do eventually pass, though, and when I'm being rational I know that, in time, they'll become even fewer and further between. It's just a case of hanging on until that happens.

The waiting lists – around the whole country, I think – are so long that it was more than a year before I got the six therapy sessions I was entitled to under the NHS, and I wanted to make sure I didn't waste a moment of any of them. 'I get so frustrated with myself,' I told the therapist during one of my appointments. 'I desperately want to start working again and to feel better than I do … And I'm so *sick* of crying,' I added, as I felt the tears pricking my eyes yet again.

'I know that's how you feel, but you must be kinder to yourself,' the therapist said. 'You're doing really well, Alice. Particularly considering the hell you've been through, you're making really good progress. You're talking about what happened, which you couldn't do at all a few weeks ago, and you're looking at new career opportunities. I understand that you want to be able to snap your fingers and have everything back the way it was before you met him. But you know it's going to take time. You *will* get there, though. You can be confident of that.'

I smiled at her through my tears and nodded my head. I was lucky to have been given a therapist I really liked. Talking to her made me feel less isolated, and less angry with myself. And it was encouraging to hear a professional person say that I wasn't to blame for what had happened, and that Joe's reaction and behaviour weren't normal.

'I know,' I said, dabbing at my tears with a tissue from the box she held out to me. 'It's just that, on some days, the doubts creep back in and I feel worthless and stupid again. Then I blame myself for what happened, even though I know you're right and Joe's behaviour wasn't my fault.'

It wasn't long after the last of my sessions with the therapist that I applied for a job. Until then, just the thought of having to go for an interview and tell people, 'This is me,' filled me with panic.

It wasn't easy going back to London the first time 'after Joe'. Everything there seemed to remind me of him and of the life I'd had before I met him. In fact, I was so anxious about the interview that I arrived ridiculously early, and I was sitting in a café, killing time and trying to calm my nerves, when two girls came in and sat at the table next to mine. They were probably in their early twenties, and one of them was telling the other one about the internship she was doing, how well it was going and how she hoped it would lead to a proper job.

Suddenly, I felt a terrible pang of jealousy and for a moment I thought I was actually going to cry. They were both so young and full of optimism, so certain that anything was possible and that, whatever happened, their lives were going to be fun. But as I listened to them, I began to realise that it was their attitude I was really jealous of, because even if reality didn't end up meeting their expectations, they'd adapt and still be happy. 'And that's what I have to do,' I thought. 'What happened during the months I spent with Joe is irrevocable – the wounds will heal, but the scars will probably remain forever. I can't change the past. But the future can be whatever I want it to be.'

When I came out of the job interview a couple of hours later, I phoned Sarah, whom I'd arranged to meet when she finished work.

'I had to force myself not to phone you,' she told me. 'How did it go?'

'Good, I think. I was dreading it, but it seemed to go quite well. In fact, I found myself enjoying it. It felt really good to be doing something normal at last, something that might help me get my life back. I know it sounds stupid, but it felt like Joe hadn't won after all.'

'It doesn't sound stupid,' Sarah said. 'I'm so proud of you, Alice. I know you want that job, but even if you don't get it, it's been worth doing the interview. It took a lot of courage to do what you've done today. I can get off work in about an hour. I'll treat you to dinner this evening, to celebrate. Take my word for it, you're going to be more successful and, more importantly, far happier than he'll ever be.'

After I'd spoken to Sarah on the phone, I went to the National Gallery, where I sat on a bench opposite my favourite painting, Vermeer's *Young Woman Seated at a Virginal*, and thought about what it would be like to be working again, and to be happy. A couple of bored-looking teenagers in school uniform meandered past me while I was sitting there. Then an elderly woman sat down on the bench beside me and started rummaging through her handbag. And another woman took out a pad of paper and began to sketch the painting next to my Vermeer. They were all normal people doing normal things. And, for the first time in more than two years, so was I. Suddenly, I felt as though I was back in the real world, from which I'd been absent for far too long.

I did get the job, and I've been working in London for several months now. I do sometimes feel a bit resentful about the fact that, throughout everything that happened, Joe kept his job and has become quite a respected expert in his field, whereas I'm working in a different industry from the one I used to work in, and have had to start very close to the bottom rung of a ladder again. But that's fine. I'm back in London, living in a flat with a friend, and putting my history of art degree to good use. More importantly, I'm making my own life.

I'm making contact with friends again too, although only very tentatively. In fact, I bumped into a friend from university just a few days ago – a girl called Katie – while I was standing at a bus stop. The last time I'd seen her was just before I met Joe. Then I lost her contact details – along with those of almost all the other friends I had at that time – when he made me smash up my mobile phone and change my number.

When I met Katie at the bus stop, she asked me what I'd been doing for the last couple of years, and when I told her, very briefly, I was upset. She was really nice, and said she'd thought *something* must have happened when I didn't answer any of her text messages, but that she hadn't known how to get in touch with me. She's still friends with some of the other people I lost contact with, and she's going to arrange for us all to meet up, as soon as I let her know I feel able to do so. So that's something good from the past that, fortunately, hasn't been lost forever.

One of the main reasons for telling my story is the hope that it might serve as a warning to other potential victims of people like Joe. I expect most people who read it will believe that nothing similar could ever happen to them, or to anyone they know. I thought that too. I'd read stories in newspapers and magazines about women who had been subjected to horrendous psychological and physical abuse at the hands of their husbands or partners – and about men who'd been abused by women. But, in my mind, it was something that happened to *other* people, people who weren't able to take care of themselves for some reason, who weren't very good judges of character or didn't have families and friends to turn to when things started to go wrong. I didn't consider for even a moment the possibility that it could ever happen to sensible, strong, career-focused women like me.

In fact, figures for England and Wales that were released by the Office of National Statistics in 2015 show that one woman is killed every three days by a past or present partner. In addition, one in four women will experience domestic abuse during their lifetime. And, according to the Home Office, domestic violence has a higher rate of repeat victimisation than any other crime. So maybe it *is* happening to someone you know, someone who has been so brainwashed and is so frightened they'll deny it, and won't accept any help that might be offered to them.

I thought at the time that I resented the attempts my family and friends made to help me. I told myself they didn't understand what Joe and I were going through, and that I needed to do the things he was telling me to do so that I could make him better. I wish now that I had been honest with them, or that I had taken the advice of the woman who spoke to me outside the café in London that day and told me, 'You've got to leave him.'

Deep down inside me somewhere, I think I always knew the truth about my relationship with Joe. But I was in denial, because I was frightened and because I had been essentially brainwashed into believing the lies he told me so convincingly. What I needed was for someone to tell me the truth again and again – that it was not my fault, that Joe's behaviour wasn't acceptable, that I wasn't alone and did have a way out – until, eventually, I was forced to accept it.

It was very difficult for my family and friends to keep trying to intervene when I kept insisting that I was all right and didn't need their help. But I did need it, because I was too weak and scared to extricate myself from the situation that, eventually, only the people who really loved me could see for what it was.

To anyone who recognises any aspect of their own situation in my story, I would say, 'Don't wait. Leave now. You don't have to live like that. It isn't your fault. And it won't get better.' And to anyone who knows someone they think is being manipulated, coerced and abused by their partner: 'Keep in touch with them, however difficult they make it for you to do so. And don't be put off by their apparently heartfelt but ultimately unconvincing denials.'

A few months after Joe told me it was over, my doctor said to me one day, 'You were lucky to have got out when you did, Alice. You're very fortunate to be alive.' I think that was when it finally hit me just how serious my situation had been.

I used to feel sick with fear whenever Joe shouted at me, 'I will kill you if you move, if you scream, if you speak. Believe me, Alice, I *will* kill you.' And I did believe him. Every time it happened, I'd think, 'Is this the last time? Will he really do it this time?' Then I'd wake up the next morning determined to phone my sister, my best friend, my parents, even the police, and beg them, 'Please help me. You were right: his behaviour isn't normal. He's a madman and I do, desperately, need help.'

But as the relief of finding myself still alive slowly began to fade, my determination to leave always faded too. For a while, Joe would be vulnerable and charming – although never apologetic – and I would accept his assertion that he was the injured party, not me. And when he told me, as he always did, that he *needed* me to stay, because I was the only person who could help him get through the agony of hurt I'd caused him, I'd feel guilty again. I'd put cold water on the bruises and bite marks he'd inflicted on me so viciously the night before, and I'd abandon any thought of leaving, because it *was* my fault and, because, for some reason, I had to believe that, eventually, if I tried hard enough, everything *would* be all right.

So when my doctor said I'd been lucky, I realised, at last, that he was right and that I had come incredibly close to dying at the hands of the charming, funny, kind man I'd loved, a man who is, in reality, a potentially dangerous psychopath.

About the Author

Alice Keale is 34 and lives in London, where she is working hard to establish herself in a new career. She is also slowly rebuilding all the other aspects of the life she lost after she met and fell in love with the man of her dreams.

Jane Smith is the ghostwriter of numerous bestselling books, including several *Sunday Times* top ten bestsellers. www.janesmithghostwriter.com

Moving Memoirs

Stories of hope, courage and the power of love…

If you loved this book, then you will love our Moving Memoirs eNewsletter

Sign up to…

- Be the first to hear about new books

- Get sneak previews from your favourite authors

- Read exclusive interviews

- Be entered into our monthly prize draw to win one of our latest releases before it's even hit the shops!

Sign up at

www.moving-memoirs.com